Cuthbert

and the
Northumbrian
Saints

An Introduction to the Saints of the
Northumbrian Golden Age
from the Baptism of King Edwin to the
Death of Bede
c.627-735 AD.

Paul Frodsham

NORTHERN
HERITAGE

Published in association with
The Golden Age of Northumbria Project

First published in the United Kingdom in 2009 by Northern Heritage Publishing.

Northern Heritage
Units 7&8 New Kennels, Blagdon Estate, Seaton Burn,
Newcastle upon Tyne NE13 6DB
Telephone: 01670 789 940
www.northern-heritage.co.uk

Text copyright:
© 2009 Paul Frodsham

Design and layout:
© 2009 Ian Scott Design

Printed and bound in China by 1010 Printing International Ltd.

British Library Cataloguing in Publishing Data
A catalogue record for this book is available from the British Library.

ISBN 978-0-9555406-3-9

Acknowledgements

For help at various stages during the production of this book the author and publisher are grateful to Derek Sharman (The Golden Age of
Northumbria Project), Tom Cadwallender (Northumberland Coast Area of Outstanding Natural Beauty), Anne Heywood (Durham Cathedral),
Sharon Thompson (Bede's World), Jonathan Butler (English Heritage), Sandra Powlette (British Library), Stan Beckensall, Ivan Lapper and
Diane Anderson.

Cover images
Main photograph of Bamburgh Castle and Inner Farne by Gavin Duthie
(used here by kind permission of the Northumberland Coast Area of Outstanding Natural Beauty).
Image of Cuthbert's cross © The Chapter of Durham Cathedral.

Contents

1
From the Dark Ages to the Golden Age
An introduction to the world of Cuthbert and the northern saints

Durham Cathedral is an icon of north-east England. It is one of the world's most magnificent buildings, a fact reflected in its status as a World Heritage Site. Yet it would simply never have existed without St Cuthbert, a seventh-century saint of the Northumbrian Golden Age. But who was St Cuthbert? And what was the Northumbrian Golden Age? This book attempts some answers, providing an overview of the Golden Age, biographies of its most important saints, and, in a brief concluding section, a consideration of the relevance of the Golden Age to twenty-first century life in north-east England.

St Cuthbert's tomb, Durham Cathedral. (© The Chapter of Durham Cathedral/ Jarrold Publishing).

After more than three centuries of occupation, the Roman army, and with it Roman administration, departed from Britain in the early fifth century. The following couple of centuries are generally known as the 'Dark Ages', about which we know little but during which local dynasties of warrior-aristocrats fought amongst themselves for influence within the power vacuum left by the departing Romans. This was the time of the legendary King Arthur who supposedly fought to defend the native British people from aggressive incomers from the continent. Whether or not King Arthur ever really existed cannot concern us here, but the fifth and sixth centuries were certainly turbulent times, involving much bloody conflict between numerous

Durham Cathedral towers majestically above the River Wear.

Statue of Constantine, York Minster.

petty kingdoms across the length and breadth of Britain.

The Northumbrian Golden Age arose out of a unique combination of interlinked religious and political circumstances during the seventh century. These can appear complicated, but in essence they arose from the competition between, on the one hand, the Roman and the British (Celtic) Churches, and, on the other, between the royal dynasties of the Anglian sub-kingdoms of Bernicia and Deira which were combined within the kingdom of Northumbria.

To understand the religious context, we must return briefly to Roman Britain. It was under Roman rule that Christianity first appeared in Britain, probably introduced as one of a number of cults practiced within the army, spreading from military establishments out into the towns and countryside of the province. Following the conversion of the Emperor, Constantine the Great, in 312, Christianity became more popular throughout Britain. Constantine had been declared Emperor while in York in 306, and York would play a key role in early British Christianity. We know that a Bishop of York was in place as early as 314, suggesting that the Church in northern England was already well organised by this

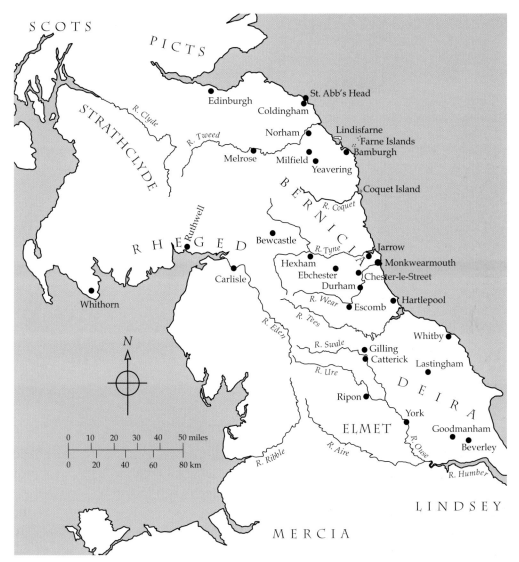

SCOTS

PICTS

STRATHCLYDE

R. Clyde

R. Tweed

RHEGED

R. Ruthwell

BERNICIA

R. Coquet

R. Tyne

R. Wear

R. Eden

R. Tees

R. Swale

R. Ure

R. Ribble

R. Aire

R. Ouse

R. Humber

DEIRA

ELMET

LINDSEY

MERCIA

Edinburgh

St. Abb's Head

Coldingham

Norham

Lindisfarne

Farne Islands

Bamburgh

Melrose

Milfield

Yeavering

Coquet Island

Bewcastle

Jarrow

Hexham

Monkwearmouth

Carlisle

Ebchester

Chester-le-Street

Durham

Whithorn

Escomb

Hartlepool

Whitby

Gilling

Catterick

Lastingham

Ripon

York

Goodmanham

Beverley

N

0 10 20 30 40 50 miles

0 20 40 60 80 km

Map showing significant kingdoms and places in the Northumbrian Golden Age.

time, probably with churches and clergy spread throughout the region. However, there is very little we can say for certain about this early Church; despite some claims (for example, at Housesteads on Hadrian's Wall) no definite Roman churches have been excavated and only a few Christian objects, such as gravestones, have been recognised from this early period throughout Northumbria.

During the fifth and sixth centuries north-east England saw an influx of pagan

Anglo-Saxons from across the North Sea, and by the mid sixth century a new Anglian aristocracy had assumed control of Northumbria. In the year 547, Ida landed at Bamburgh and took control of Bernicia, extending northward from the Tees to cover Northumberland and south east Scotland. To the south, the kingdom of Deira (covering Yorkshire) was also under Anglian rule. Ida's grandson, Aethelfrith, conquered Deira, thus creating the formidable new kingdom of Northumbria (literally, 'the land north of the Humber'). Edwin, rightful king of Deira, was forced into exile and in 603 his sister was married to Aethelfrith, thus uniting the Bernician and Deiran dynasties. Aethelfrith's military strength gained him control of much of Scotland, north-west England and the midlands, as well as his Northumbrian heartland in what is now north-east England. Although Northumbria was now united, competition, and sometimes violent conflict, between the aristocratic dynasties of the two sub-kingdoms would be a feature of its development throughout the seventh century.

It is important to remember that at the end of the sixth century the Christian Church had two contrasting foci in Britain: Canterbury and Iona. Having lost virtually all influence in Britain following the collapse of Roman rule in the early fifth century, the Roman Church was re-introduced by Augustine, sent by Pope Gregory in 597 to establish an archbishopric at Canterbury and begin the conversion of the pagan Anglo-Saxons. In contrast, the British or Celtic Church, which had developed in relative isolation from the Roman Church of mainland Europe, had its spiritual home on the Isle of Iona, at the monastery set up by the exiled Irish prince, Columba, in the 560s. Both Churches were Christian, but differed from each other in certain fundamental details including the method of calculating the date of Easter – the single most important date in the Christian calendar. The organisation of the two Churches was also very different; the Roman Church operated a heirachical system of bishops and archbishops, all of whom owed allegiance to the Pope. The British Church, in contrast, consisted of a large number of relatively independent monasteries ruled by abbots or abbesses. Only at Whithorn (near Wigton in the extreme west of the kingdom) do we have clear evidence of a pre-existing British church surviving into the Northumbrian age. Whithorn, claimed to be 'Scotland's first Christian Community', is traditionally thought to have been founded by St Ninian (Scotland's first saint) in 397; in the eighth century it became a Northumbrian bishopric but is not associated with any of the great Golden Age saints so cannot be considered in any detail here (though anyone interested in early Christianity should without doubt pay a visit to the Whithorn Story Visitor Centre).

If Christianity had gained a foothold in the north-east during Roman times, then it seems soon to have faded away; it certainly had no place in Aethelfrith's world. In 616, Edwin, himself still a pagan at this stage, returned to the north-east and defeated Aethelfrith in battle, assuming control not just of Deira but of the whole of Northumbria. From Canterbury, the Roman Church gained a foothold here when Edwin married the Kentish princess, Aethelburh, in 625. Edwin was subsequently converted and baptised by Aethelburh's chaplain, Paulinus, at York in 627. Edwin was eventually succeeded by Oswald, son of Aethelfrith, who had spent Edwin's reign in exile in Scotland where he had become a devout member of the British Church. Oswald invited Aidan, from Iona, to set up a new monastery in the British tradition on Lindisfarne; this replaced York as the spiritual centre of the Northumbrian kingdom. The inconsistencies between the two Churches came to a head in the 660s, when King Oswiu (like his brother, Oswald, a member of the British Church) married Edwin's daughter, Eanflaed, who, having spent Oswald's reign in exile in Kent, was firmly allied with the Roman Church. King and Queen, both devout Christians, thus celebrated Easter as much as four weeks apart, a situation which could not be allowed to continue.

Bamburgh Castle (© Gavin Duthie/Northumberland Coast AONB). The medieval castle stands on the site of Ida's sixth-century stronghold, a key site throughout the Golden Age.

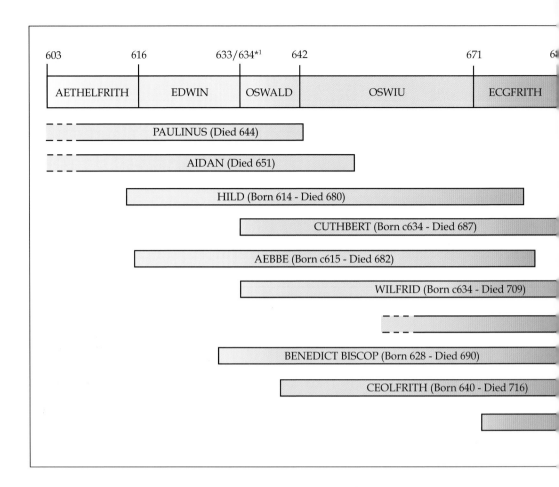

603	616	633/634*[1]	642	671	6
AETHELFRITH	EDWIN	OSWALD	OSWIU	ECGFRITH	

PAULINUS (Died 644)

AIDAN (Died 651)

HILD (Born 614 - Died 680)

CUTHBERT (Born c634 - Died 687)

AEBBE (Born c615 - Died 682)

WILFRID (Born c634 - Died 709)

BENEDICT BISCOP (Born 628 - Died 690)

CEOLFRITH (Born 640 - Died 716)

It was eventually resolved at the Synod of Whitby in 664, at which representatives of the two Churches argued their cases in front of Oswiu. Perhaps surprisingly there is no record of Cuthbert being present at this crucial gathering, and, thanks largely to the eloquence of Bishop Wilfrid, the Roman Church emerged triumphant and York again became Northumbria's pre-eminent religious centre. These momentous events in the history of Northumbria and the Christian Church are discussed more fully in subsequent sections.

Despite not infrequent periods of conflict, the reigns of Edwin, Oswald and Oswiu provided relative stability in which Christianity became firmly and irreversibly established. Kings and other members of the royal dynasties worked closely with bishops and other religious leaders; indeed many members of the Bernician and Deiran royal families themselves left secular life to join the Church. Edwin, Oswald and Oswiu, as well as being 'Bretwaldas' (effectively overlords of all the

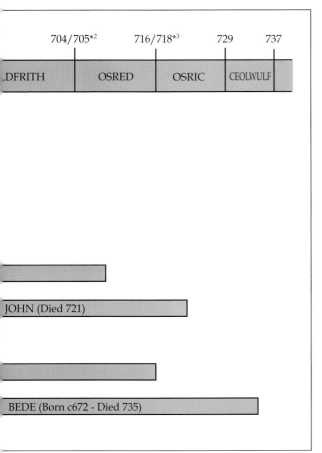

Anglo-Saxon kingdoms) on the back of their military prowess, became accepted in death as 'royal saints'. The next two kings, Ecgfrith and Aldfrith, also enjoyed great power, but during their reigns the previously dominant kingdom of Northumbria was in relative decline. Subsequent kings never approached the three Bretwaldas in terms of their influence throughout Britain, and Northumbrian power declined from the late seventh century as political infighting led to a series of short-lived reigns; during the eighth century Northumbria had no less than fifteen kings, several of whom were assassinated or exiled.

However, as Northumbrian political power waned, the Church continued to thrive. In addition to its God-given spiritual power, gifts of land from Oswald, Oswiu and other kings ensured that it became phenomenally wealthy in financial terms. It was this wealth that underlay the development of the Northumbrian Golden Age. No-one can say for sure when the Golden Age started or when it

Oswiu: window in St Andrew's Church, Heddon-on-the-Wall.

Ninth-century gravestone from Lindisfarne, thought to depict Viking warriors on one face and the Day of Judgement on the other.

finished, but for the purposes of this book our starting point is the baptism of King Edwin, in 627, and we will follow the story through until the death of Bede in 735. The Golden Age certainly extended past Bede and on throughout most of the eighth century. Conventionally, its end is marked by the first Viking Raid on Lindisfarne in 793, but some historians see it as continuing well into the ninth century, although after 793 the monasteries and churches existed under the constant threat of further Viking raids. By the late ninth century, Deira was ruled directly by Vikings based at York, and Bernicia, although nominally independent and ruled from Bamburgh by an Anglian aristocracy, owed allegiance to Scandinavian overlords. The once great kingdom of Northumbria would never recover, though aspects of its Golden Age would continue to influence life in the region through until the present day.

This book does not seek to provide a comprehensive history of Anglian Northumbria, but to present an overview, within its historical context, of the world of Cuthbert and the other Northumbrian saints, all of whom lived and died during the seventh and early eighth centuries and were written about by Bede. Indeed, Bede is very much our main source for information about these characters, although we should note at this early stage that much of what he wrote was not

history as we know it today; he was a deeply religious man whose writings were largely concerned with Christianity, and his work merges accounts of historical events with those of miracles in a way that we would regard today as rather unprofessional. This, however, is not a criticism; we must remember that he lived and worked at a time when scientific explanations of natural phenomena that we take for granted today simply did not exist. Bede undertook much scientific study himself, but still explained much of what went on in the world by reference to acts of God.

Regardless of any inspiration or spiritual fulfilment they may have received through the new religion, it is doubtful whether most people in seventh or eighth-century Northumbria thought of themselves as living in a Golden Age. The story of the Golden Age is primarily about royalty and the Church, while the vast majority of Northumbrians lived out their lives as peasants, working the land and paying rent to the landed aristocracy who in turn supported the king. The king relied on the support of his landholding aristocrats (known as 'thegns') for military service when required, rewarding them with a share of the wealth of newly conquered lands. There was a constant need for kings to maintain their armies as competing dynasties sought to extend their areas of influence throughout Britain. Warriors naturally tended to side with the most powerful of these dynasties; the loyalty of his warriors was essential to the success of any king, but loyalties could change as the fortunes of each dynasty fluctuated. To an extent the nature of this 'heroic age' is encapsulated within the ancient story of Beowulf; history was made largely by the actions of powerful kings and warriors.

There was, however, a crucial difference between seventh-century Northumbria and Beowulf's eighth-century Scandinavia; the presence of the Christian Church. The key institutions in the development of the Golden Age were the monasteries, of which the most important to our story is Lindisfarne. We will consider individual monasteries, including Wearmouth/Jarrow, Whitby, Tynemouth, Hartlepool, Coldingham, Beverley, Ripon and Hexham, in subsequent sections. For now, we must concentrate on a general overview of their relevance to the Golden Age.

The monasteries were set up by Kings and Queens who granted them substantial estates for the production of food and other resources. They were ruled by abbots

Spectacular ruins of the medieval monastery stand on the site of Aidan's original monastery on Lindisfarne.

Medieval ruins on the sites of Golden Age monasteries: Whitby (left) and Tynemouth (above).

or abbesses who were themselves often members of the royal family. The monasteries, and the priors (deputy abbots) monks and nuns who served within them, therefore owed allegiance to the royal family as well as to God. The early Celtic monasteries consisted of a timber church surrounded by small timber dwellings for the monks and nuns and other buildings including workshops, stores, a guesthouse, hospital, school and scriptorium. Several of the early monastic sites were later occupied by fine medieval churches, some of which remain in use today while others (such as Lindisfarne, Tynemouth and Whitby) survive as spectacular and atmospheric ruins. The monasteries were centres of learning, where young monks and nuns could gain knowledge of many subjects in addition to Bible studies.

Craftsmen within the monasteries combined influences from Celtic (Irish), Anglian and Roman sources to produce often exquisite artefacts. One of the most iconic examples is Cuthbert's pectoral cross of gold and garnet, but many other beautiful objects were also made. Magnificent books were produced in the scriptoria, of which by far the most famous is the Lindisfarne Gospels. This stunning volume, made in honour of God and St Cuthbert, combines Celtic, Anglo-Saxon and Mediterranean artistic influences. It probably dates from the

The Lindisfarne Gospels: carpet page from the Gospel of Matthew (reproduced by courtesy of the British Library).

The Franks Casket (replica on display at Bede's World, Jarrow).

period 715-720 and was apparently the work of Eadfrith, appointed Bishop of Lindisfarne in 698. Long before the introduction of paper, its pages are of vellum (calf-skin), and its production used the skins of some 130 calves, presumably reared on the monastery's extensive estates. The Franks Casket, another icon of the Golden Age, was intricately carved from whalebone somewhere in Northumbria soon after 700. It merges Mediterranean Christian imagery, Jewish history, Roman mythology and Germanic legend in a single extraordinary object.

While the earlier, Celtic monasteries had timber churches, after the Synod of Whitby craftsmen were brought over from the continent to build magnificent stone churches, often using masonry plundered from old Roman sites. Escomb in County Durham is a fine surviving example, built with stone plundered from the nearby Roman fort of *Vinovia* (Binchester). These churches had stained glass windows, and their interiors were embellished with wonderful stone carvings, colourful wall paintings and embroidery. Chalices, plates and other furnishings were of gold and silver, reflecting the great wealth of the Church which continued to attract valuable gifts from the Northumbrian nobility.

The Church's stonemasons produced splendid stone crosses, standing up to six metres high, which were erected not just at the monasteries but also at churches and other far-flung locations throughout the kingdom. Sadly, few of these survive intact today, but surviving fragments demonstrate that they were wonderful works

Above: Escomb Church.
Right: Inside Escomb Church

of art, incorporating intricate detail which is impossible for most people to draw, never mind carve in stone. Most would originally have been brightly painted, making them no less dramatic in appearance than the illuminated pages of the Lindisfarne Gospels and other contemporary manuscripts. While these manuscripts would have only been seen close up by the men and women of the Church, the crosses could be seen and appreciated by everyone. Some fine examples of cross fragments are on display in Durham Cathedral library, while others can be inspected at churches and museums throughout the region.

The following account is structured around the most famous Church men and women of the Golden Age, each of whom is discussed within his or her own section. A number of events (eg the Synod of Whitby) and characters (eg Kings and Queens, some of whom themselves became saints) are woven into these accounts, inevitably appearing in more than one section. While a case could be

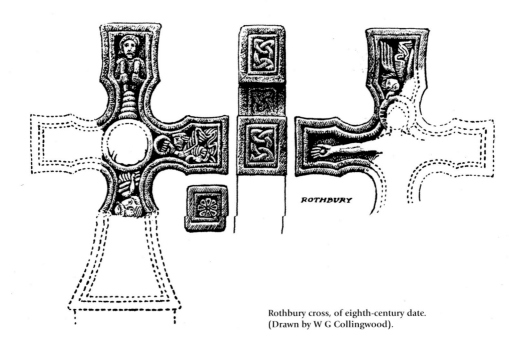

Rothbury cross, of eighth-century date.
(Drawn by W G Collingwood).

made for giving some of the most famous kings (most notably Edwin, Oswald and Oswiu) their own sections, this would have necessitated excessive repetition so, while acknowledging their key roles within our story, they are considered within the sections about Paulinus, Aidan and others. Several other Golden Age saints are denied more detailed attention here due to lack of space. For example, St Cedd, born into a noble Northumbrian family in about 620, founded a royal monastery at Lastingham (North Yorkshire) and did much important work in London, Essex and East Anglia. His younger brother, St Chad, served as Abbot of Lastingham and, briefly, as Bishop of York, but is best known for his work in Mercia and Lindsey as Bishop of Lichfield, even though he only filled this position for the three years prior to his death in 672. St Acca (c660-742), loyal companion of Wilfrid and his successor as Bishop of Hexham, and also a close friend of Bede, is another who could legitimately claim a section of his own but who has not been granted it on this occasion. The same is true of St Finan and St Colman, Aidan's successors as Bishop of Lindisfarne. St Alcuin of York was a prolific writer much concerned with education, and played a key role in the expansion of Northumbrian learning and influence throughout Europe; however, he was born at about the time of Bede's death, so is not considered further here.

Details of Rothbury cross shaft.

LINDISFARNE

Arguably the most fascinating of all the Golden Age saints is Eanflaed, the first Northumbrian Christian known to history. As the daughter of King Edwin, the wife of King Oswiu and the mother of King Ecgfrith, and also as Abbess of Whitby, she played a key role in the story of the Golden Age. Her life must have been extraordinary and her name is mentioned several times in the following pages, but on balance it was decided not to give her a section of her own within the book (though she is currently the focus of a research project by the writer that will hopefully be published separately in due course). Eanflaed's daughter, Aelfflaed, although also denied her own section here, is currently enjoying considerable fame through her key role in English Heritage's on-site interpretation of Whitby Abbey.

Having set the scene, we will now consider the lives of the main Northumbrian saints, their role within the Golden Age, and their impact on subsequent history. We must remember that we know very little about these people, other than information provided by Bede who, with the best will in the world, cannot always be described as impartial with regard to religious matters. Stained glass windows depicting the saints may be considered attractive, but they are products of their own time rather than of the Golden Age; for example, this

Acca's Cross, Hexham Abbey, thought to have marked the head of Acca's grave.

volume features several windows in St Andrew's Church, Heddon-on-the-Wall, which dates originally from the seventh century, but the windows were added in 1921. In reality we know next to nothing about what the various Golden Age characters looked like, and must rely on often scanty archaeological evidence to reconstruct the world in which they lived. Nevertheless, and regardless of one's views on Christianity, the fascinating story of the Golden Age is an essential aspect of English history and is well worth telling.

St Paul's, Jarrow; the site of the monastery where Bede produced the wonderful books that are so crucial to our understanding of the Golden Age. (© Rector and Warden of St. Paul's Church, Jarrow/Bede's World).

Paulinus: window in
St Andrew's Church,
Heddon-on-the-Wall.

2
St Paulinus

While Aethelfrith of Bernicia exercised power over the whole of Northumbria, Edwin, who considered himself the rightful heir to the throne of Deira, found refuge at the court of the East Anglian King Raedwald. Raedwald was immensely powerful and was later recorded as having been 'Bretwalda' (a title applied retrospectively, in the ninth century, to those few kings thought to have exercised overlordship over most if not all of Britain's Anglo-Saxon kingdoms). The fabulous ship burial from Sutton Hoo, near Ipswich in Suffolk, is thought by many to have been his final resting place, although this cannot be proved beyond doubt. Raedwald had been converted to Christianity, but reverted to paganism; Edwin must have discussed matters of religion with him, although the extent to which his thinking may have been influenced by Raedwald is not known.

Aethelfrith attempted to bribe Raedwald into handing Edwin over, presumably in order to have him killed and thus extinguish his claim to the Deiran crown. Raedwald, who by this time may well have struck up a firm friendship with Edwin, refused, and instead marched north with a huge army to defeat and kill Aethelfrith at the 'Battle on the Idle' (near Retford, Nottinghamshire) in 616. Edwin, with the backing of Raedwald, thus became king not just of Deira but of the whole of Northumbria. Aethelfrith's children were now banished and fled north, though three of them (Oswald, Oswiu and Aebba) were destined to return and play key roles in the development of the Golden Age. Edwin enjoyed great military success, incorporating parts of North Wales and the Isle of Man into his kingdom.

While Raedwald was alive, Edwin remained traditionally pagan in his religious views, but things changed after Raedwald's death in about 620. Edwin inherited Bretwalda status, assuming power over all the English kingdoms except Kent which seems to have retained a large degree of independence. In 625, Edwin sought to extend his influence over Kent, not by military conquest but through marriage to Aethelburh, sister of the Kentish King Eadbald. This marriage was

SAINT · EDWIN

crucial to the introduction of Christianity to Northumbria, as Aethelburh, a devout Christian in the Roman tradition, was accompanied to Northumbria by her Italian chaplain, Paulinus, who was to have a profound influence over Edwin. Paulinus is one of the few Golden Age personalities for whom we have a physical description. Bede records that he was a 'tall man with a slight stoop, who had black hair, a thin face and a narrow aquiline nose, his presence being venerable and awe-inspiring.'

On Easter Day, 626, Edwin was the victim of an assassination attempt orchestrated by Chuichelm, King of Wessex. He survived the attempt and that very night Aethelburh, perhaps brought into premature labour by the trauma of the day's events, gave birth to a daughter, Eanflaed. Edwin thanked his pagan gods for the safe delivery of his daughter, but Paulinus told him he should be thanking Christ. Badly wounded by the would-be assassin, Edwin decided that if God would grant him life and victory over Chuichelm, he would, according to Bede, 'renounce his idols and serve Christ; and as a pledge that he would keep his word he gave his infant daughter to Paulinus to be consecrated to Christ.

Edwin: window in St Andrew's Church, Heddon-on-the-Wall.

All Hallows Church, Goodmanham, possibly on the site of the pagan shrine destroyed by Coifi.

Accordingly, on the Feast of Pentecost this infant, together with twelve others of her household, was the first of the Northumbrians to receive Baptism.'

In due course, Edwin recovered from his wounds and marched his formidable army south seeking revenge against Chuichelm. He was successful and Chuichelm accepted subservience to him. Upon his return to Northumbria, Edwin summoned his advisors, including Paulinus, to his main Deiran palace (at an as yet undiscovered location near the Derwent, probably close to the village of Sancton) and, after a lengthy debate, announced his decision to become a Christian. Coifi, the chief pagan priest, willingly rode out from the palace to

Above and right: York Minster, almost certainly on the site of Paulinus' original Northumbrian church.

destroy the ancient pagan shrine at Goodmanham (possibly on the site now occupied by Goodmanham Church), and a new timber church was built in York where Paulinus was installed as Bishop of the entire Northumbrian kingdom. The extent to which Edwin's eventual conversion was influenced by political expediency rather than genuine religious fervour must remain forever unknown. The church certainly helped him administer his vast and expanding kingdom, and helped to provide a banner under which all the people could unite. It also provided ready access to a network of potentially advantageous political alliances, not just within Britain but extending to Gaul and Rome. Whatever his motives, he was baptised by Paulinus at York on Easter Day 627. The timber church where this momentous event took place, within the ruins of the old Roman fort of *Eboracum*, was later transformed into a great stone church; today the site is occupied by the magnificent medieval cathedral of York Minster.

Bede describes the years following Edwin's baptism as wonderfully peaceful, recording how the king rode around the kingdom and was greatly loved and

respected by his people. Edwin's kingdom was vast, and he spent much of his time travelling; he is traditionally credited with the founding of Edinburgh ('Edwin's fort') in 626. There were several royal centres throughout the kingdom which he would visit from time to time, spending time feasting and consulting with his thegns. Sometimes, he was accompanied by Paulinus, and Bede tells us about one such occasion at the royal site of *ad Gefrin* (Yeavering) in the northern Cheviots. Here, the distinctive hill known as Yeavering Bell, which towers above the site of *ad Gefrin*, seems to have acquired special significance long before Golden Age times. Four thousand years ago, a number of late Stone Age ceremonial monuments were aligned upon it, and its summit is crowned by the largest and most spectacular prehistoric hillfort in Northumberland, perhaps built in about 1000BC. The ancient power of this special place was appropriated by the Anglian aristocracy, and a royal palace seems to have been established here by the late sixth century, probably during the reign of Aethelfrith. The site was rediscovered by aerial photography in 1949, and a brilliant campaign of excavation by the Cambridge University archaeologist Brian Hope-Taylor in the 1950s and 1960s enables us to reconstruct much of its history. The site was burnt to the ground twice, apparently during raids by Cadwalla and Penda, but was rebuilt on each occasion. Its structures included a great hall (not unlike Beowulf's *Heurot*), a great enclosure (presumably for cattle and perhaps horses), and a unique open-air timber theatre within which people could assemble to be addressed by king and bishop. In its earliest phase, *ad Gefrin* had a pagan temple, but by the time of its abandonment, probably a few years before 700, it had a Christian church with an extensive graveyard. Nothing of *ad Gefrin* survives above ground today, but the site remains hugely atmospheric and is well worth a visit.

Whether things during Edwin's reign were ever actually as peaceful as Bede implies must be open to serious doubt. Bede wishes to paint a picture of peace and harmony following Edwin's conversion, but in reality Edwin was a warrior king and the threat of violence was ever present. He was killed, along with his son Osfrith, on 12th October 633 at the Battle of Hatfield Chase, near Doncaster, while seeking to fight off an invasion by Cadwalla of Gwynnedd and Penda of Mercia who were fighting against Northumbrian overlordship. His second son, Eadfrith, was taken by Penda and put to death at a later date, thus creating disorder regarding the legitimate heir to the Northumbrian crown. (We should note that

Reconstruction of Yeavering by Peter Dunn, showing part of the 'great enclosure' in the foreground, the great hall, and the 'theatre' from which a group is being led down to the River Glen for baptism. (© English Heritage).

The monument at Yeavering, commemorating Paulinus' presence here in 627.

there is some confusion over the actual year of Edwin's death; Bede gives the year 633 but some historians claim it was a year earlier. The date is important in providing a framework for subsequent events, such as the accession of Oswald; here we will follow Bede in dating Edwin's demise to 633).

Bede tells us that Edwin's head (presumably severed from his body by the enemy, either during or in the aftermath of the battle of Hatfield Chase) was buried within his church in York. Another source states that his body was initially buried at a chapel close to the battle site, traditionally thought to be Edwinstowe in Sherwood Forest, but that this location was not sufficiently prestigious for the long term burial of Northumbria's first Christian king whose body was later reburied in the monastery church at Whitby.

Had Edwin not died in 633, things may have been very different, as Pope Honorius intended to establish an archdiocese at York with Paulinus as archbishop. In the event, following Edwin's death, Paulinus fled by sea back to Kent, taking with him the remnants of the royal family, including Queen

Aethelburh and her infant daughter Eanflaed. Eanflaed would later return to Northumbria to play an important role in our developing story, but Paulinus never returned, becoming Bishop of Rochester until his death on 10th October 644. In the twelfth century, the great medieval cathedral of Rochester was built on the site of the Anglo-Saxon church and Paulinus' relics were transferred to a beautiful silver shrine, a popular place of pilgrimage throughout medieval times.

Paulinus' only recorded accomplice in Northumbria was James the Deacon, who stayed behind after Edwin's death to continue preaching throughout the north. It is possible that other priests also remained, but there were very few churches and Christianity's hold on the kingdom must have been tenuous in the extreme.

Cadwalla may have traced his ancestry back to the rulers of Brynaich, the British precursor of Bernicia, and may thus have regarded himself as the legitimate ruler of at least the northern portion of Northumbria. Regardless of this, his invasion was presumably fuelled largely by a desire to reinstate British rule and the British Church to Northumbria, in place of the Anglian aristocracy and Roman Church of Edwin and Paulinus. A large part of his motivation must have been revenge for Edwin's earlier invasion of Gwynedd (including the taking of Anglesey), as a result of which he was forced into temporary exile, probably in Ireland. Whatever the explanation, he was despised by Bede, who tells us that 'showing no mercy even to women and innocent children, he tortured all to death with bestial savagery, and for a long time spread havoc throughout the land, intending to wipe out the entire English race from the land of Britain.'

After perhaps a few months, Cadwalla seems to have returned to Wales, with Northumbria splitting back into its two ancient kingdoms. Deira was ruled by Osric, a cousin of Edwin, and Bernicia by Eanfrith, eldest son of Aethelfrith. Both Osric and Eanfrith abandoned Christianity in favour of ancient pagan tradition, but neither had much influence on subsequent proceedings as Cadwalla returned within a year to kill them both. He then 'occupied the Northumbrian kingdoms for a whole year, not ruling them like a victorious king but ravaging them like a savage tyrant, tearing them to pieces with fearful bloodshed.' The Northumbrian stage was now ready for the dramatic return of Oswald, and through him the arrival of Aidan.

3
St Aidan

St Aidan has been described as the 'apostle of all England', and his influence on the adoption of Christianity throughout the land was immense. He could not, however, have been so successful working in isolation, and to understand his impact we must also consider the roles of King Oswald and King Oswiu, with both of whom his story is inextricably linked.

Throughout Edwin's reign, Oswald had been exiled amongst the Scots and Irish, and had been baptised into the Celtic Church at the monastery on Iona, founded by Columba in 563. Following the deaths of Eanfrith and Osric, Oswald returned to Northumbria in 634 to claim his rightful crown from Cadwalla. His army must have been a mixture of Christians and pagans, united in their desire to defeat the 'tyrant' Cadwalla, but on the night before the battle Oswald erected a timber cross and ordered all his men to pray before it. This hugely symbolic event, regarded by many as the point at which Christianity became permanently established in Northumbria, is thought to have taken place at the appropriately named Heavenfield, on the line of Hadrian's Wall 5km north of Hexham. Bede tells us that monks from the monastery at Hexham built a church on the site and that many miracles occurred here. Today, a church of St Oswald still occupies the site, and although this dates back only to 1737 it is quite possible that buried remnants of an earlier structure survive somewhere in the vicinity.

On the morning after Oswald's men had knelt and prayed before the cross at Heavenfield, Cadwalla's army was duly routed and Cadwalla himself was killed. The fighting seems to have extended over the wild moors south of Hadrian's Wall, and Bede tells us that Cadwalla was killed 'at a place called in English Deniseburn', thought to be the Rowley Burn, in the valley of the Devil's Water near Whitley Chapel, about 5km south of Hexham. Following this enormously significant battle, Oswald became king of a re-united Northumbria, eventually

Statue of Aidan, Lindisfarne Priory.

following Edwin in achieving Bretwalda status.

With his position militarily secure, Oswald turned his attention to the spiritual well-being of his people. Many had renounced Christianity following Edwin's death, and Oswald sent to Iona for a missionary who would reverse this trend. The first man sent from Iona failed in his task, according to Bede because he was too strict and the people disliked him. In his place was sent Aidan, who arrived in 635 to become Bishop of Lindisfarne, a role he would fill until his death sixteen years later. The windswept island of Lindisfarne, within sight of the royal palace at Bamburgh, must have reminded both Oswald and Aidan of Iona. It was now to play a fundamental role in the conversion of the kingdom of Northumbria, spending three decades as the kingdom's most important religious centre, more important even than York.

Oswald and Aidan worked closely together, Aidan providing spiritual guidance for the king who gave large grants of land and money to the Church. History has been kind to Oswald, recording him as a most generous Christian king. Bede records that one Easter, while feasting with his thegns in the presence of Aidan, he gave a silver dish and food to the poor who had gathered outside his hall.

View over the Devil's Water, south of Hexham, where Cadwalla was killed by Oswald's forces in 634.

Generous as Oswald may have been to his own people, we should note that Edwin's Christian widow was so fearful for the safety of her young children during his reign that she sent them abroad to live in exile with the King of the Franks. Clearly, she thought that Oswald, given the chance, would have had them permanently removed from the scene to ensure that none of Edwin's descendents could ever return to claim the Northumbrian crown.

Aidan was not fluent in the Anglian (Old English) language, and Bede tells us that Oswald would sometimes accompany him, acting as translator. We may note here that most of the population of Northumbria, especially in the more remote regions, still probably spoke a British language at this time, and may have understood Aidan without great difficulty; it would presumably have taken several generations for the ancient British language to have been fully replaced throughout the kingdom by the English tongue of the new aristocracy. It may have been Aidan's ability to communicate with the masses that underlay his popularity. He was apparently very popular with everyone, from peasant to royal family, and even (despite the differences between the two Churches) with bishops of the Roman Church in southern England. Bede tells us that he walked rather than rode around the kingdom, taking time to talk with people he met on his travels.

Oswald had destroyed Cadwalla's army, but not Penda's. While Cadwalla returned to Northumbria in 634 and met his death, Penda spent time consolidating his position at home in Mercia. However, Penda's ambitions in Northumbria were far from satisfied. He continued to attack Northumbria, on one occasion seeking to burn Bamburgh to the ground.

Oswald: window in Durham Cathedral.

Fortunately, Aidan was watching from Farne and he prayed for the wind to change direction, which it obligingly did, fanning the flames towards Penda's troops who duly fled!

The threat from Penda, however, did not subside. In 642, at 38 years of age and after eight years in power, Oswald was killed in a battle against the combined armies of Mercia and Powys, apparently at Oswestry in Shropshire. According to legend, his head and arms were hacked from his body and displayed on stakes, eventually to be recovered by Oswiu (Oswald's brother and eventual successor as Bretwalda) who gave the head to Lindisfarne Church and took the arms to his royal residence at Bamburgh Castle where they were buried, presumably within the Church of St Peter. The rest of his body was eventually buried at the monastery of Bardney (Lincolnshire), which became a focus for many miracles and a major pilgrimage site as the cult of St Oswald grew in popularity. In the tenth century his remains (minus head and arms) were seized by the Mercians and rehoused within the crypt of the royal priory church of St Oswald, Gloucester, which on account of its great wealth and the many miracles associated with its resident saint came to be known as the 'Golden Minster'. This in turn became a great pilgrimage centre, but during the eleventh century it was eclipsed by the ancient Abbey of St Peter (now Gloucester Cathedral). In 1152, St Oswald's became an Augustinian Priory, surviving until the Dissolution in 1537. What happened to Oswald's relics after this is not known.

When the church on Lindisfarne was abandoned in the face of the Viking threat in 875, Oswald's skull was placed for safekeeping in Cuthbert's coffin; it was still there when the coffin was placed within Cuthbert's shrine in Durham Cathedral in 1104. This is why traditional medieval images of Cuthbert, for example in paintings and on stained glass windows, depict him holding the head of Oswald. When Cuthbert's coffin was opened in 1827, pieces of a skull displaying evidence of a massive and clearly fatal sword blow across the brow were found alongside his skeleton. This fragmentary skull, which must surely

Reconstruction by Peter Dunn of Aidan's monastery on Lindisfarne (© English Heritage).

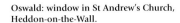
Oswald: window in St Andrew's Church, Heddon-on-the-Wall.

have been Oswald's, presumably still lies within Cuthbert's tomb. Oswald's arms may await discovery within the buried remains of St Peter's Church, Bamburgh Castle, although there is a rumour that his right arm was removed to Peterborough in the tenth century.

In death, Oswald became a very popular saint and is the patron of more than fifty ancient English churches. He is often depicted with a raven, and according to legend kept a pet raven that performed duties such as delivering the ring on his wedding day and recovering one of his arms from the battlefield after his death. Ancient pagan tradition links the raven, a bird of ill omen, with the battlefield, where it fed on the bodies of the slain. Oswald's raven is clearly a reflection of his success as a warrior, and is a good example of ancient pagan imagery being appropriated within Christian tradition.

After Oswald's death, his brother Oswiu became the third of Aethelfrith's sons to rule Bernicia, but Deira was controlled by Oswin, a cousin of Edwin. Both kings enjoyed close relationships with Aidan, which must have posed problems for the bishop as both

were in political competition with each other. Bede tells us that Oswin was a generous and humble king, of whom Aidan was particularly fond.

Oswiu sought to reimpose Bernician rule over the whole of Northumbria. In 643, with this ambition very much in mind, he took Eanflaed (the daughter of Edwin who, as we have already seen, had fled as an infant to her mother's kingdom of Kent on her father's death a decade earlier) as his second wife. This helped to

Above: **Statue of Aidan, Lindisfarne Priory Museum.**
Left: **Aidan: window in St Mary's Church, Lindisfarne.**

+In memory of Edward de Stein Knight 1887-1965 and Miss Gladys de Stein 1891-1968 +

cement Oswiu's relations with the powerful kingdom of Kent, while also giving further weight to his claim for control over Deira. The risk of war between Bernicia and Deira grew ever greater, and conflict was only averted through the betrayal of Oswin who was killed by forces loyal to Oswiu somewhere near Gilling (North Yorkshire) in 651. Oswiu, perhaps out of genuine guilt and remorse, and probably influenced by Eanflaed and Aidan, later founded a monastery at Gilling where prayers were said daily for Oswin. Traditionally, Oswin is said to have been buried at the monastery at Tynemouth, where he was venerated as a saint and many miracles were attributed to him. His relics were translated into the medieval monastery church at Tynemouth Priory in 1110, but their present whereabouts are unknown.

After the murder of Oswin, Oswiu appointed Aethelwald (a son of Oswald) as his client king in Deira, but he still faced a serious threat from the mighty Penda who stepped up his violent campaign to incorporate Northumbria into his pagan kingdom of Mercia. Oswiu strengthened his position through political alliances with kings in southern England (including Penda's own son) and through these alliances the Celtic Church expanded into the south. Eventually, Oswiu's forces managed to defeat and kill Penda at the Battle of Winwaed (near Leeds) in 655. This gave Oswiu

Tynemouth Priory, on the site of the early medieval monastery where Oswin was buried.

control of Mercia, enabling him to follow in the steps of his brother, Oswald, as Bretwalda. After his defeat of Penda, Oswiu gave much land and money to the Church, and many new monasteries were founded throughout Northumbria. It was during Oswiu's twenty-eight year reign that Christianity became irreversibly

St Aidan's Church, Bamburgh.

established throughout the kingdom.

Aidan did not live to see the elevation of Oswiu to Bretwalda, as he died on 31st August 651, just twelve days after Oswin. He had spent sixteen years as the first Bishop of Lindisfarne, during which he had taught many who would take up influential positions within the developing Church throughout Britain, as well as providing spiritual guidance to two of Northumbria's greatest ever kings. Aidan died at his church at Bamburgh which then became the focus for many miracles. He was succeeded as bishop by Finan, Colman, Tuda, Eata, and eventually Cuthbert. Aidan was buried in the Lindisfarne monastic cemetery, but was soon moved by Finan to lie beside the altar in a newly built monastic church which

Bede tells us was 'of hewn oak, thatched with reeds'.

Some of Aidan's bones were taken back to Iona by Colman, following his resignation as Bishop of Lindisfarne after the Synod of Whitby in 664. When the monks eventually fled Lindisfarne in 875, Aidan's remaining bones were placed, along with Oswald's skull, in Cuthbert's coffin. What happened to them subsequently is not recorded; they may have been amongst the 'extra' bones recorded in Cuthbert's tomb when this was opened in the nineteenth century. There is no real evidence to support the tradition that his relics were removed to Glastonbury Abbey, although a shrine to him did exist there in medieval times. Despite the claims of Glastonbury, Aidan remains very much a Northumbrian saint; his own church at Bamburgh, rebuilt in the thirteenth century, remains a focus for Christian worship and is generally regarded as one of Northumberland's finest parish churches.

Bamburgh Castle from St Aidan's churchyard.

Saint Hilda

4
St Hild

St Hild (known from medieval times as 'Hilda') was a Deiran princess, being a great niece of King Edwin. Born in 614, probably in East Anglia while her parents were in exile during the reign of Aethelfrith, she moved to Northumbria sometime after 616 when Edwin had become king. She was baptised into the Roman Church by Paulinus at the same time as Edwin in 627, but was also greatly inspired by Aidan and the Celtic Church.

Hild spent the first half of her life on a secular basis within the royal household, but in 647, at the age of 33, she was invited by Aidan to establish a new religious community, the exact location of which is unknown, on the banks of the Wear. A year later she transferred to the monastery at Hartlepool where she was made abbess, staying here until 657. Hartlepool was a very important and respected establishment, and it was here that Aelfflaed, infant daughter of King Oswiu and Queen Eanflaed was passed into Hild's care 'to be consecrated to God in perpetual virginity'. Little is known of the subsequent history of the monastery

Left and above: Images of Hild from windows in St Hilda's Church, Hartlepool.

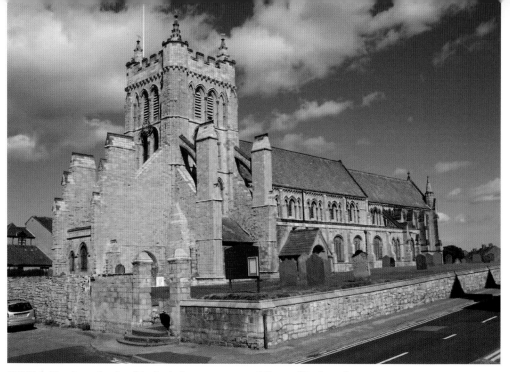

St Hilda's Church, on the site of the Anglo-Saxon monastery of *Heruteu* (Hartlepool).

at Hartlepool, but archaeological discoveries from various locations across the headland suggest that it continued to thrive throughout the seventh and eighth centuries. Archaeologists have unearthed remains of timber buildings, burials which appear to come from three separate cemeteries, evidence of metalworking, and copper pens which were presumably used in the monastery's scriptorium. Nothing is known of the abandonment of the monastery, but there is no evidence for any buildings having been sacked or burnt by Vikings; the monastery was probably abandoned in the face of the Viking threat towards the end of the ninth century and its timber buildings simply left to rot in the ground. Today, the mightily impressive medieval Church of St Hilda stands close to, if not actually on, the site of the original monastery church.

In 657, Hild moved to the newly founded double monastery at Whitby, taking the young Aelfflaed with her. Double monasteries, quite common at this time, consisted of separate groups of monks and nuns united under an abbess. Under Hild, Whitby enjoyed a great reputation for learning; several bishops (including St Wilfrid and St John of Beverley) studied here before moving on to influential positions elsewhere. Bede tells us that Hild was held in high regard by everyone,

Inside St Hilda's Church, Hartlepool.

CAEDMON

DAVID

HILD

OEDMON

TO THE GLORY
OF GOD AND IN
MEMORY OF
CÆDMON
THE FATHER
OF ENGLISH
SACRED SONG
FELL ASLEEP
HARD BY 680

and that kings and princes came to Whitby to seek her advice on many occasions. Whitby is also famous for Caedmon, a humble cowherd who gained a miraculous talent for poetry and music via a dream, subsequently composing much religious verse, in Anglo-Saxon rather than Latin, which became very popular within the Whitby community and elsewhere.

Parts of Whitby's seventh-century monastery were excavated in the 1920s, but sadly the excavations were not well conducted and the results are in many ways unclear. The remains of several small timber buildings were uncovered, along with fascinating finds including decorative objects of silver, copper and jet, writing tools, cooking pots, loom weights, combs, pins, and carved stones. Clearly, much of Hild's monastery remains underground for future archaeologists to investigate.

As abbess of the monastery, Hild oversaw one of the key events in the development of Northumbrian Christianity; the Synod of Whitby in 664. This was held to discuss the relative merits of some contrasting characteristics of the

Left and below left: Twentieth-century stone cross at St Mary's Church, Whitby, featuring Caedmon.

Below right: Tombstones, including some of Anglo-Saxon date, found during the 1920s excavations at Whitby Abbey.

Whitby Abbey, on the site of Hild's seventh-century monastery.

Celtic and Roman churches, the most significant of which was the method of calculating the date of Easter. The synod was attended by King Oswiu and many important churchmen from throughout the land. After many speeches and much consideration, Oswiu's verdict was in favour of the Roman Church. One may wonder to what extent this decision was made on strictly religious grounds, rather than factors such as the political and economic advantages on offer from the wealthy Church of Rome, but from this point on it was the Roman Church that would govern religious life in Northumbria.

Hild endured a painful illness during the final six years of her life, but continued to pray and teach at Whitby. She died in 680, aged 66, and was presumably buried at Whitby where we may reasonably assume a shrine to her would have been set up by her joint successors, Eanflaed and Aelfflaed. The monastery church of St Peter at Whitby became the favoured burial site for the Northumbrian royal family; Edwin's body was reburied here, to be joined in due course by those of Oswiu, Eanflaed, Aellfflaed and others. Remarkably, the excavations in the 1920s recovered what seems to be part of Aelfflaed's tombstone. More recent excavations in 1999 and 2000 uncovered part of a massive cemetery, containing more than 1000 graves, which was in use during the eighth and ninth centuries.

The monastery at Whitby survived almost two centuries after Hild's death, eventually being abandoned, under threat from Viking attacks, in 867. Today, the site is occupied by the impressive ruins of Whitby Abbey, itself abandoned following Henry VIII's Dissolution of the Monasteries in 1539.

Fragment of inscribed stone thought to be from Aelfflaed's tomb, found during the 1920s excavations, Whitby Abbey.

Cuthbert holding the
head of Oswald:
window in
St Andrew's Church,
Heddon-on-the-Wall.

5
St Cuthbert

It may legitimately be argued that within their lifetimes Paulinus, Aidan, Wilfrid and others all played roles no less significant than Cuthbert's in the development of Northumbrian Christianity. Nevertheless, in death, it was Cuthbert who rose to prominence, and it is Cuthbert who is most fondly remembered and most widely revered today.

Cuthbert's origins are obscure. We know nothing of his parents; some claim he was of aristocratic birth, others that he was from a peasant family. We know that he was born in about 634 and brought up from an early age by a widow called Kenswith. He was an active and intelligent child, and at the age of 16 was working as a shepherd in the hills near Melrose when, according to Bede, he had a vision of Aidan's soul being borne to heaven by angels; a vision which occurred at the very moment of Aidan's death. This vision led him to enter the monastery at Melrose.

What we know of Cuthbert comes largely from the Anonymous Life of Cuthbert, written shortly after his death, and also two Lives (one in prose and the other in verse) provided by Bede. Bede's accounts clearly use the earlier Life, but embellish it with more detailed discussion of various miraculous tales. Some of these tales are rather bizarre, and must surely have been made up long after the events were supposed to have taken place. There is one, for example, that refers to Cuthbert having been rather mysteriously addressed as 'Holy Priest and Bishop' while still a young child. Another explains how, while walking on the cliffs near the monastery at Tynemouth, he observed a group of peasants mocking some monks who were on a boat being blown out to sea. Cuthbert prayed for the wind to change direction, which it duly did and the monks were brought safely back to land; the peasants, embarrassed by their actions, at once accepted Christianity and from this moment never ceased to praise Cuthbert. (This story recalls the way in which Aidan miraculously changed the wind direction to save Bamburgh from the fires ignited by Penda's troops). Whether or not we choose to regard such miracles as historically authentic, they intrigue us because they relate to real places that we can still visit today. At Tynemouth, we can wander around the site of the monastery known to Cuthbert and Bede, now dominated by the ruins of the medieval monastery and castle, and observe boats out at sea in the same general location as that referred to in the above story. Excavations at Tynemouth have uncovered remains of timber buildings from the seventh-century monastery, possibly buildings that would have been visited by Cuthbert, and also fragments of decorated stone crosses and grave markers. However, as with so many of the old monastic sites, there is frustratingly little that we can say for certain about Tynemouth.

Cuthbert transferred from Melrose to Ripon, but problems arose from the fact that Ripon was a Roman, rather than Celtic, institution and he soon returned to Melrose where he became prior. He travelled widely throughout Bernicia, on foot like Aidan before him, preaching the gospels to the most remote upland communities. Some of these may have been visited previously by Aidan, or perhaps even Paulinus, but Cuthbert seems to have had even more success in convincing people to take up Christianity.

In 664, after the Synod of Whitby, Cuthbert became Prior of Lindisfarne, where

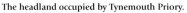

The headland occupied by Tynemouth Priory.

Hobthrush Island (St Cuthbert's Island), Lindisfarne.

he was charged along with the abbot, Eata, with introducing Roman rule to the previously Celtic establishment. While he may have felt some resentment at this task, given his own Celtic background, he apparently undertook his duty with enthusiasm, spending his time teaching and training the monks, studying and praying, and preaching out in the community. Cuthbert, however, longed for absolute seclusion, enabling quiet contemplation and prayer, and, with the blessing of the abbot, he retired in 676 to a cell on the tiny Hobthrush Island (now St Cuthbert's Island) just offshore from the monastery.

Longing for still greater isolation, Cuthbert moved in his early forties to Inner Farne, five miles south of Lindisfarne and a mile offshore from the royal fortress of Bamburgh. Here he built a hermitage, surrounded by a wall that blocked out views of everything except the sky, where he would sit and contemplate, his gaze drawn upwards to the sky and to heaven. He wished to be self-sufficient, and grew his own barley; when the birds ate the seed he instructed them to stop, which they duly did. He was very fond of local wildlife and there are stories linking him with otters, dolphins and other wild creatures; the local eider ducks are still referred to today as 'Cuddy's ducks' in his honour. Despite living in such isolation, Cuthbert did not cut himself off entirely and was in constant demand for his wisdom and advice. He had a guesthouse built on Inner Farne, at some

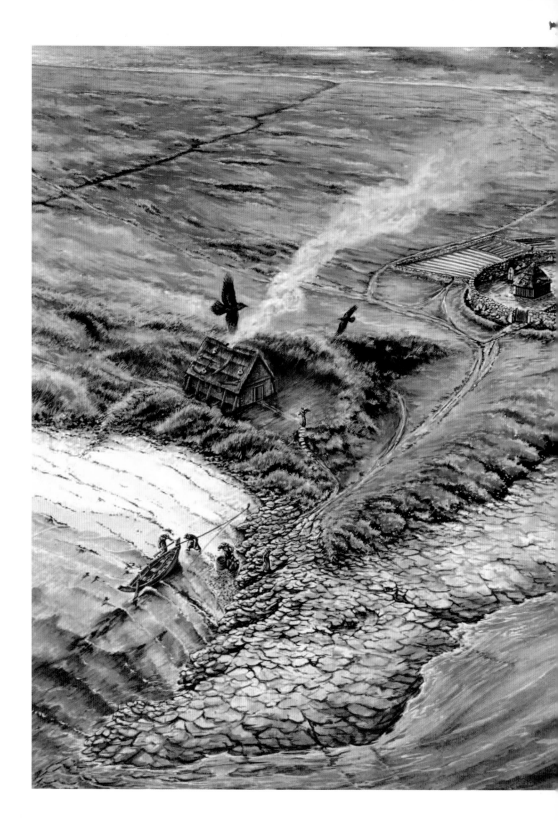

Speculative reconstruction of Cuthbert's cell on Inner Farne, by Peter Dunn. (© English Heritage).

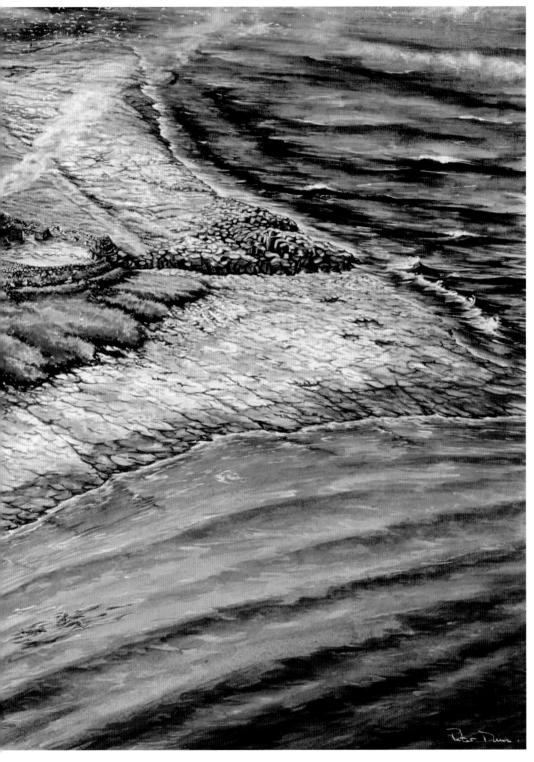

distance from his cell, where he would meet people who wished to consult with him. He exerted huge influence over the kingdom of Northumbria, and was consulted directly on occasions by members of the royal family.

In 684, the Archbishop of Canterbury, Theodore, presided over a synod at 'Twyford' (probably Alnmouth), at which it was decided to appoint Cuthbert as Bishop of Hexham. Cuthbert, however, refused, preferring the solitude of his hermitage on Farne. King Ecgfrith personally visited him on Farne to try and convince him to accept the role. Eventually, he agreed to become a bishop, but apparently not of Hexham; Eata, Bishop of Lindisfarne, agreed to swap positions, and Cuthbert thus became Bishop of Lindisfarne in 685. Unsurprisingly, we are informed that he was a perfect bishop, being associated with several miracles in addition to carrying out his everyday duties with distinction.

One of Cuthbert's duties as bishop was to act as advisor to the king. Following an ill-advised and brutal invasion of Ireland in 684, Ecgfrith, against the advice of Cuthbert, marched his army north to attack the Picts. Having ignored his bishop's advice, aged 39 and after fifteen years on the Northumbrian throne, Ecgfrith was killed while fighting the Picts at the battle of Nechtanesmere (near

Bamburgh Castle and Inner Farne. (© Gavin Duthie/Northumberland Coast AONB).

Forfar) in May 685. He was succeeded by his half-brother Aldfrith, who ruled Northumbria until 705. Aldfrith was the illegitimate son of Oswiu and an Irish princess named Fin. He had spent much of his youth in Ireland and on Iona, and was a great collector of books. Sometimes referred to as the 'Scholar King', he is credited with no great military achievements and exercised power over an area much reduced from that dominated by his predecessors. We may imagine that Aldfrith and Cuthbert would have had much in common, given their love of the Celtic Church and their interest in books and the pursuit of knowledge.

Cuthbert died on 20th March 687, a couple of months after resigning as bishop and returning to his beloved Inner Farne. His death, however, is far from the end of his story. He was initially buried in a stone coffin beneath the floor of the Church of St Peter at Lindisfarne, but in 698 his body was exhumed to be placed in a newly built sepulchre within the church. This was normal practice at the time for the most revered holy men, who would be buried in the ground for a few years to allow their flesh to decay, after which their bones would be recovered and placed in an above-ground tomb within a church which could be visited by pilgrims. This act of 'elevation' was effectively a declaration of sainthood. Cuthbert's elevation was extraordinary as his body was found to be intact after

St Cuthbert's Chapel, Inner Farne, dates from the fourteenth century but appears to incorporate masonry from an earlier structure. (Photo: Andrew Hayward/Northumberland Coast AONB).

more than a decade in the ground; a fact regarded by the monks as a clear indication of his sanctity. Throughout the next two centuries pilgrims came from far and wide to pray at Cuthbert's shrine, many receiving apparently miraculous cures for a variety of ailments.

In 793, the church and monastery on Lindisfarne were sacked by Vikings, but Cuthbert's remains were unharmed. The monks rebuilt the monastery, but, even though Lindisfarne was not actually attacked again, the threat of further raids was ever present. Documentary sources suggest that Cuthbert's relics may have been moved inland to Norham for a while in the mid ninth century, but the evidence is far from clear. Eventually, in 875, the risk was deemed too great and the monks decided to abandon the monastery, taking Cuthbert's coffin (which, in addition to Cuthbert's remains, also included Oswald's head and some of Aidan's bones) along with other treasures including the Lindisfarne Gospels, with them. Cuthbert's coffin was moved from place to place for nearly a decade before the monks opted to settle at Chester-le-Street in 883.

The monks who travelled with Cuthbert and guarded his relics during his eight years on the move became known as the 'Community of St Cuthbert'. Of course, travelling around northern England for eight years with a dead body and assorted other relics in a wooden box must have proved logistically rather awkward, and it is probable that tales of his wonderings are largely symbolic rather than historically accurate. Regardless of this, the Community became increasingly wealthy on the basis of the extensive lands owned by the Church and the new gifts that the cult of Cuthbert continued to attract. This wealth, coupled with the popular devotion of the people to 'their' saint, gave the Community growing economic and political power. Throughout the turbulent times of the ninth, tenth and eleventh centuries, the Community of St Cuthbert survived by forging relationships and alliances at various times with kings and earls of Northumbria, Scandinavian kings in York, kings of Wessex, kings of Scotland, and the Normans under William the Conqueror.

Cuthbert's love of wildlife is reflected in this window in Durham Cathedral.

Despite a lack of clear archaeological or documentary evidence, most Northumbrian monasteries are thought to have been abandoned in the face of the Viking threat during the latter half of the ninth century. In 876, the aggressive Halfdan assumed power and proceeded to reallocate much of Northumbria to his followers, but the Community of Cuthbert somehow managed to survive and even to grow in influence.

Halfdan's successor, Guthred was sympathetic towards Christianity, being buried within York Minster on his death in 894 or 895. He granted the Community of Cuthbert much land between the Tyne and the Tees, enabling a 'permanent' home for Cuthbert to be created at Chester-le-Street. A church was built here on the site of the old Roman fort of *Concangium*, and for 112 years this served as the cathedral of the Northumbrian kingdom, a huge diocese extending from coast to coast across central Britain, and north as far as Edinburgh. Despite the confiscation of much land by Ragnald in about 920, the community still retained extensive landholdings throughout the north-east and became gradually wealthier and more powerful.

Due to the presence of Cuthbert's shrine, Chester-le-Street became a great pilgrimage centre, visited by kings and commoners from far and wide. In one famous incident, in about 934, King Athelstan (grandson of Alfred the Great of Wessex, and effectively king of all England) came to Chester-le-Street on pilgrimage and placed several gifts with Cuthbert's relics. A decade later, King Edmund did likewise, also confirming the rights and privileges of the Community of St Cuthbert. King Cnut followed in 1031, presenting further gifts of land to the Community. Aside from any genuinely religious motivation, it was in the interests of

The lid of Cuthbert's coffin.

66

Cuthbert's Last Journey: sculpture by Fenwick Lawson in St Mary's Church, Lindisfarne.

KATHLEEN OPHIR PARBURY 1901-1985

such leaders to align themselves with the vast and growing religious, economic and political power of the Community of St Cuthbert, thus earning public approval throughout northern England in the face of constant threats from further north.

It was at Chester-le-Street that the priest, Aldred, added his Anglo-Saxon translation to the Lindisfarne Gospels, writing literally 'between the lines' of the original Latin, thus producing the first ever translation of the gospels into 'English'. Today, the site of the ancient cathedral of Chester-le-Street is occupied by the eleventh-century Church of the Virgin Mary and St Cuthbert, within which can be seen a fine late nineteenth-century stained glass window depicting the story of the Lindisfarne Gospels and also a splendid facsimile copy of the Gospels. Visitors to the church should also inspect the medieval Anker's House, a small museum containing several fragments of Anglo-Saxon sculpture.

In 995, faced with possible threats from Scotland and Scandinavia, Cuthbert was moved temporarily to Ripon, and from there to Durham where, other than a brief

Cuthbert: window in St Mary's Church, Lindisfarne.

Cuthbert: bronze cast of sculpture by Fenwick Lawson, Lindisfarne Priory.

return to Lindisfarne in 1069/70 to escape William the Conqueror's 'harrying of the north', he has remained ever since. Durham has a quaint foundation myth (featuring a vision provided by Cuthbert and the recovery of a lost cow: the 'Dun Cow') but the decision to settle here must surely have been made on more practical grounds. It seems to have resulted from an alliance between the Community of St Cuthbert and Uchtred, Earl of Northumberland. Nothing is known of the history of the peninsula prior to the arrival of St Cuthbert in 995, when Uchtred apparently made land available for a new church at what was presumably a pre-existing settlement.

Initially, a simple timber church was built to house Cuthbert's coffin. This church was soon replaced by the *Alba Ecclesia* (the 'White Church', presumably of timber with whitewashed wattle and daub walls). Within three years, on 4th September 998, a fine stone church, the *Ecclesia Major*, was consecrated. Here, Cuthbert's shrine was visited by William the Conqueror in 1071. The cult of St Cuthbert continued to grow in popularity, and in 1093, work began on the present cathedral which incorporated a splendid new shrine behind its high altar. Cuthbert's coffin was transferred to this new shrine in 1104, after which the *Ecclesia Major* was demolished (no sign of it survives above ground, although remains of it may lie buried beneath the present cathedral cloisters).

Cuthbert continued to play a major role throughout the complex and often turbulent medieval history of

Church of St Mary and St Cuthbert, Chester-le-Street.

Durham. In medieval times, Bishops of Durham, although still very much accountable to the English Crown, enjoyed a considerable degree of independence. Known as the 'prince-bishops', they governed the extensive lands of St Cuthbert as a palatinate and became extremely wealthy. Cuthbert himself remained very popular with everyone. In about 1175, a Durham monk named Reginald compiled a list of miracles associated with Cuthbert in the three centuries from 875; the total was 141, and given that most occurred in the vicinity of his shrine, this gave further impetus to Durham as a pilgrimage centre, thus bringing further fame and wealth to the cathedral and the Community.

It was noted in 1104 that Cuthbert's body, apparently seen by several monks, was still intact. Also inside the coffin at the time were the head of Oswald, the bones of Bede, and 'some treasure' (no mention is made of any of Aidan's bones, despite the fact that they had supposedly been placed in the coffin back in 875). Cuthbert is often depicted holding the head of Oswald, and

71

St Cuthbert's tomb in Durham Cathedral.

the link with ancient royalty was probably a significant factor underlying the importance and affection accorded to Cuthbert by later kings. A beautifully leather-bound Gospel of St John dating from about 698, the oldest manuscript anywhere in Europe to retain its original binding, was removed from the coffin in 1104 and is now in the British Library in London. Following completion of the magnificent Chapel of the Nine Altars in 1280, the shrine of 1104 was redesigned, being raised from the floor and expensively embellished with gold and green marble. Sadly, at the Dissolution in 1538 this was dismantled and stripped of its gold, silver and jewels by the King's Commissioners. Following the Dissolution, the cathedral was refounded in 1541, and Cuthbert's body, reportedly mummified and still intact, was reburied in 1542 in a vault on the site of the destroyed shrine.

Durham Cathedral, founded to house the body of St Cuthbert.

St Cuthbert's pectoral cross of gold and garnet. (© The Chapter of Durham Cathedral).

In 1827, the contents of this vault were examined by the cathedral librarian, James Raine, a respected local historian and antiquarian, along with other cathedral staff. Cuthbert's remains were recorded on this occasion as a skeleton, wrapped in silk and a shroud. They were contained within three coffins, the innermost of which was fragmentary but has been restored and can be seen today in the exhibition of Cuthbert's relics in the cathedral treasury. This is thought to be the original coffin in which Cuthbert's body was laid to rest within the church at Lindisfarne in 698, and which was subsequently moved around the north-east by the Community of St Cuthbert after its removal from Lindisfarne in 875. Its decoration incorporates imagery from Mediterranean, Irish and Anglo-Saxon tradition. Also recovered from the tomb in 1827 were Cuthbert's magnificent pectoral cross of gold and garnet, incorporating a white shell inlay from the Red Sea or Indian Ocean, a liturgical comb of African elephant ivory, and a portable wooden altar covered with silver; all of these are thought to have been buried with Cuthbert on Lindisfarne in 698. Twelve centuries later, in 1899, the tomb was again opened, and following expert medical examination the bones within it were pronounced in all probability to be those of Cuthbert.

Cuthbert's name was removed from Durham Cathedral's official dedication in the sixteenth century, but was restored in 2005; the cathedral is now officially dedicated to 'Christ, Blessed Mary the Virgin and St Cuthbert'. Cuthbert would no doubt be humbled to find himself in such exulted company, but given the chance would perhaps be happy to walk away from the grandeur of Durham and back to the seclusion and simplicity of his little hermitage on Inner Farne.

6
St Aebbe

Aebbe, sister of Oswald and Oswiu, became the first Abbess of Coldingham, a monastery at a remote and beautiful location on the Berwickshire coast. The site, named in honour of Aebbe, is now known as St. Abb's Head. Little is known of Aebbe's earlier life; prior to her appointment to Coldingham she is rumoured to have founded a nunnery at Ebchester in County Durham, but we have no proof that such an institution ever actually existed. Coldingham monastery was founded on land given by King Oswiu in 655, and was the most northerly of all the Northumbrian monasteries. Bede tells us that it was a magnificent monastery, but nothing of it remains to be seen today. There are some low earthworks at the traditional site, known as Kirk Hill, but these appear to

Looking north along the coast towards the site of the Coldingham Monastery, St Abb's Head.

belong to a later structure, perhaps a medieval chapel. Despite the lack of visible remains, the site is well worth visiting for the fabulous views along the Northumbrian coast towards Lindisfarne which, perhaps significantly, is just visible on the horizon on a clear day. The site lies within the St Abb's Head Nature Reserve, managed by the National Trust for Scotland.

In its early days, Coldingham was apparently a model establishment, and was

Aebbe watches over a modern gateway in St Abb's village.

Above: No visible sign of Aebbe's monastery survives today; these low earthworks belong to later structures on the presumed site.

Left: Perhaps it was here, on the coast adjacent to Aebbe's monastery, that Cuthbert immersed himself in the sea to pray.

visited by Cuthbert while he was prior at Melrose. It was here that Cuthbert was observed praying at night immersed up to his neck in the sea, in imitation of Drycthelm of Melrose who would recite psalms while submerged in the freezing waters of the Tweed. Something, however seems to have gone wrong at Coldingham in subsequent years. It is singled out by Bede on account of the indiscretion of some of its monks and nuns, who slept, ate and drank to excess and did not pray or worship in accordance with the Church's rigorous discipline.

Adamnon, a devout Irish monk at Coldingham, received news from a stranger (apparently in a vision) that the unacceptable behaviour of many at the monastery was soon to be punished in the form of a great fire that would destroy the establishment. He reported this to Aebbe, who soon improved things, but after her death in about 682 the community's discipline again slackened. The fire duly occurred, and the monastery was destroyed, never to be rebuilt. Given that Aebbe was apparently highly regarded by King Ecgfrith, Cuthbert and Bede, it is surprising to hear of stories of such unacceptable behaviour at her monastery, and why it should have occurred here remains unexplained. Perhaps she was away for

much of the time; there are suggestions that she spent much time in Wessex, where an ancient Oxford church is dedicated to her. Alternatively, could it be that the whole story was invented retrospectively to account for the disastrous fire?

It was to Coldingham that Queen Etheldreda went after the annulment of her marriage to Ecgfrith (an annulment which Ecgfrith apparently did not dispute, perhaps not surprisingly as Bede tells us that the queen maintained her virginity throughout the marriage). She received her training from Aebbe before moving on to found a new monastery at Ely. Ecgfrith stayed at Coldingham several times while travelling throughout his kingdom. On one such occasion in 681, his second wife, Eormenberg, was gravely ill; Aebbe advised the king to release Wilfrid (jailed the previous year) from custody, which he duly did, whereupon Eormenberg was miraculously cured.

In addition to St Abb's and Ebchester, St Ebba's Chapel at

Etheldreda: window in St Andrew's Church, Heddon-on-the-Wall.

Beadnell on the Northumberland coast is another site traditionally associated with Aebbe. Here, a small medieval monastery stood on the rocky promontory known as Ebba's Nook, where slight remains of a thirteenth-century chapel can still be seen. It is possible, though by no means certain, that a small monastery may have occupied the site during or shortly after Aebbe's lifetime.

Despite her apparent weak leadership at the time of the Coldingham scandal, after her death Aebbe became another of Northumbria's 'royal saints', alongside her brothers Oswald and Oswiu. She is traditionally thought to have been buried at Coldingham, but later moved to Durham where her bones were interred within Cuthbert's shrine. If true, then hers may have been some of the 'extra' bones noted within Cuthbert's tomb when it was opened in the nineteenth century.

St Ebba's Church, Ebchester, on the site of the Roman fort of *Vindomora*. A twelfth-century account claims that Aebbe founded a nunnery here, but no evidence of it has ever been found.

ST. WILFRID

In memory of
Charles Sykes
1873-1967
A gift from his wife Elsie

7
St Wilfrid

In complete contrast to the ascetic lives of Aidan and Cuthbert, Wilfrid enjoyed a lifestyle of great opulence. His was not the lifestyle of the Celtic monastery, but of the great Church of Rome. His churches were not of timber, but of stone, embellished with wonderful fixtures and fittings that reflected the grandeur and wealth of the Roman Church. Whereas Aidan and Cuthbert had travelled largely on foot, Wilfrid rode a fine horse, accompanied and protected by a personal retinue of armed bodyguards. His turbulent career involved much travel, including several trips to Gaul and Rome, and he had much influence over the development of the Church throughout England and Europe. He is credited with having introduced the Rule of St Benedict to Northumbria. Benedict, an Italian monk who lived in the first half of the sixth century, designed a set of rules for the running of his own monastery at Monte Cassino. This 'Rule of St Benedict', intended to enable close unity between man and God through a combination of obedience and poverty, became very influential throughout Europe. It describes everything from the founding and structure of a monastery to the nature of food and timing of meals. According to Benedict, monks should drink no more than half a pint of wine a day as excess alcohol 'leads even wise men into infidelity'.

Most of our knowledge of Wilfrid comes from a biography written shortly after his death, in 709, by Eddius Stephanus, a monk at Ripon. Bede also tells us much about Wilfrid, whom he certainly held in high regard, though without the degree of affection he clearly had for Aidan and Cuthbert. Wilfrid was born into an aristocratic Northumbrian family in 634, possibly also the year of Cuthbert's birth. Wilfrid and Cuthbert both dedicated their lives to the service of God, and their paths must have crossed on many occasions, but they certainly led very different lives. We are told that Wilfrid impressed Queen Eanflaed with his good looks and intelligence, and she supported him in the development of his religious career.

Wilfrid: window in Ripon Cathedral.

The medieval abbey, on the site of Wilfrid's seventh-century Church of St Andrew, dominates the town of Hexham.

Hexham Abbey. (Photo: Stan Beckensall).

As a young man, Wilfrid was tasked with caring for one of King Oswiu's trusted thanes, Cudda, who had retired to Lindisfarne because of ill health. This gave him a direct link to the royal family, while also providing the opportunity to experience monastic life under Aidan who was still Bishop of Lindisfarne at the time. Wilfrid, however, always favoured the Roman Church over the Celtic, and we may assume that he would have discussed the relative merits of the two with Queen Eanflaed on many occasions. We should recall that Eanflaed, daughter of Edwin, was the first ever Northumbrian to be baptised and spent many of her formative years in Kent, where Canterbury was the centre of the Roman Church in England.

Eanflaed supported Wilfrid's first trip to Rome in 652; the first recorded journey to Rome by anyone from Anglo-Saxon England. Such a trip was no simple undertaking in the mid seventh century and necessitated considerable planning. Wilfrid travelled first to Canterbury, where he would have met many influential people and no doubt did much studying. He eventually departed for Rome in the company of Benedict Biscop, previously a thane of King Oswiu, who had opted to take up a religious life. However, while Benedict travelled on to Rome, Wilfrid chose to spend a year at Lyons, having made the acquaintance of the archbishop. Wilfrid eventually arrived in Rome in 654 and spent several months visiting religious sites and meeting important people including the Archdeacon of Rome and the Pope.

Clearly in no rush to return home, he then spent a further three years studying in Lyons before eventually returning to Northumbria. On his arrival at York, he was welcomed by Alhfrith (son of Oswiu and his first wife, Riemneth of Rheged) who had become sub-king of Deira, though very much subject to the overall control of his father who remained King of Northumbria. Alhfrith appointed Wilfrid as Abbot of Ripon in 660, and gifted him much land and money to help run the monastery.

Wilfrid made a telling contribution to the Synod of Whitby in 664. As we have already observed, this key event was to decide once and for all on the relative merits of the Roman and Celtic Churches throughout the kingdom of Northumbria. Among its many participants, Wilfrid, Eanflaed and Ahlfrith supported Rome, while King Oswiu initially favoured the Celtic Church. According to Bede, Oswiu's decision to favour Rome was based largely on the seniority of St Peter over St Columba, but in reality it may have been greatly

Above: Reused Roman masonry, probably from Corbridge, in Hexham Abbey crypt. (Photo: Stan Beckensall).

Left: Seventh-century crypt beneath Hexham Abbey. (Photo: Stan Beckensall).

influenced by a number of more down-to-earth practical matters, enabling as it did the development of closer relations with the Archbishop of Canterbury and the Pope, as well as with the kingdoms of southern Britain. In 665, Wilfrid was appointed as Bishop of Lindisfarne, replacing Coleman who opted to return to Ireland rather than accept Roman rule after the Synod of Whitby. He travelled to Gaul to be ordained, but on his return in 666 was dismayed to find that Oswiu had appointed Chad in his place.

In 669, Chad was deposed (he later became Bishop of the Mercians, based at Lichfield) and Wilfrid was again appointed Bishop of York, this time properly consecrated by the Archbishop of Canterbury. Oswiu died in 671 and was succeeded by his son, Ecgfrith. As Bishop, Wilfrid built magnificent new churches at Ripon and Hexham, the latter, described at the time as 'without doubt the finest church north of the Alps', built on land donated by King Ecgfrith's first queen, Aethelthryth, in about 672. Although nothing of Wilfrid's churches survives above ground, the original seventh-century crypts, built beneath the altars to house and display precious relics, can still be seen within Hexham Abbey

The seventh-century Frith Stool (bishop's throne) in Hexham Abbey.

and Ripon Cathedral. Wilfrid also set about rebuilding the old stone church at York that Paulinus had founded under Edwin, remnants of which may lie buried somewhere beneath the present day York Minster.

Ecgfrith and Wilfrid did not get on at all well, perhaps in large part due to the king's concern that the bishop's wealth and influence could potentially rival the security of his own position. Apparently in league with Theodore, Archbishop of Canterbury, Ecgfrith divided the diocese of York into three portions, and new bishops were appointed for Bernicia (based at Lindisfarne), Deira (York) and Lindsey (Lincoln). Wilfrid, although guilty of no crime, was removed from office. Not surprisingly, he was not best pleased with this development and appealed to Rome, claiming that the king did not have jurisdiction to make such decisions. In 678, he set out again for Rome, travelling this time via Frisia (Holland) where he did much influential preaching, paving the way for future missionaries to continue the conversion of this previously pagan kingdom.

Wilfrid obtained the support of the Pope, Agatho, and returned to Northumbria in 680 with documents to support his reinstatement as Bishop of York. Ecgfrith's response was to lock him up in jail where he would no longer be a threat or a nuisance. Apparently acting on the advice of Aebbe (Abbess of Coldingham)

Ecgfrith released Wilfrid a year later, but did not reinstate him as Bishop of York. Wilfrid then moved to Sussex, setting up a monastery at Selsey where he stayed until 686. Following Ecgfrith's death in 685 his successor, his half-brother Aldfrith, recalled Wilfrid, restoring to him his monasteries and estates at Hexham and Ripon, and reinstating him as Bishop of York (albeit to the reduced diocese, following Ecgfrith's division of the old diocese into three). However, harmony between Aldfrith and Wilfrid did not last long, and following a number of disputes Wilfrid departed in 691 for Mercia, where he enjoyed a close working relationship with King Ethelred for a decade.

Disputes over his Northumbrian landholdings continued, and he decided once again to travel to Rome to appeal personally to the Pope. This time he travelled

Ripon Cathedral, on the site of Wilfrid's seventh-century church.

Two views of the Ripon Cathedral crypt, originally built in 672 beneath the high altar of Wilfrid's church.

with Acca (later to become Bishop of Hexham), travelling again via Frisia where he was welcomed with great enthusiasm. Arriving in Rome in 704, he obtained the support of Pope John VI, but on his return Aldfrith refused to give him back his Northumbrian estates. Aldfrith then fell gravely ill and, fearing that his treatment of Wilfrid may have contributed in some way to his illness, made it known that if he recovered he would return all Wilfrid's estates, and that if he died his successor should do likewise. He died in 704, and his son, Osred, duly gave Wilfrid back his monasteries and estates at Ripon and Hexham. Wilfrid subsequently became Bishop of Hexham in 706. His influence was, however, much reduced from his Northumbrian heyday in the 660s; whereas in 669 his diocese had been the whole of Northumbria, by 706 his area of direct jurisdiction was restricted to the lands around Hexham. He was, nevertheless, still an immensely wealthy man.

Wilfrid died in 709 at Oundle in Mercia, having made arrangements for the distribution of all his worldly goods (including much gold and silver, and other valuables) to a variety of benefactors including the poor of Northumbria, the abbots of Ripon and Hexham, and churches in Rome. He was buried within Ripon Cathedral, and soon after his death Ripon became established as a popular pilgrimage centre; Cuthbert's remains rested here briefly in 995 en route to Durham. There is a rumour that Wilfrid's remains were relocated to a shrine within Canterbury Cathedral in the mid tenth century, but another rumour states that it was a later bishop, and not Wilfrid, who was mistakenly removed to Canterbury. Either way, Ripon claimed still to house Wilfrid's relics and in the twelfth century work began on a new minster to house them; the relics were transferred to a shrine within this new minster in 1224. Rumour has it that Wilfrid's skull was encased in gold and enshrined separately behind the high altar. Ripon, based on the cult of Wilfrid, remained a wealthy pilgrimage centre through until the Dissolution, when his shrine was destroyed.

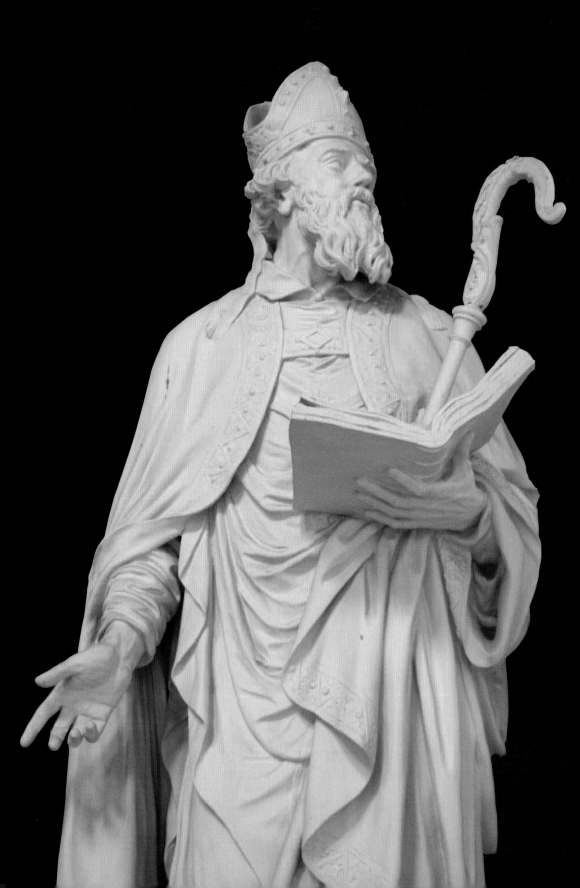

8
St John (of Beverley)

John of Beverley enjoyed a distinguished career in the Church. Reputedly born at Harpham (near Driffield), he studied at Whitby under Hild and at Canterbury. He was made Bishop of Hexham in 687, and Bishop of York in 705, before retiring to his own monastery at Beverley where he died in 721. While Bishop of Hexham, he ordained Bede as a deacon (in 691) and as a priest (in 702); it is perhaps no surprise that Bede writes about him with great fondness.

John enjoyed a reputation for the miraculous healing of the sick. Bede provides

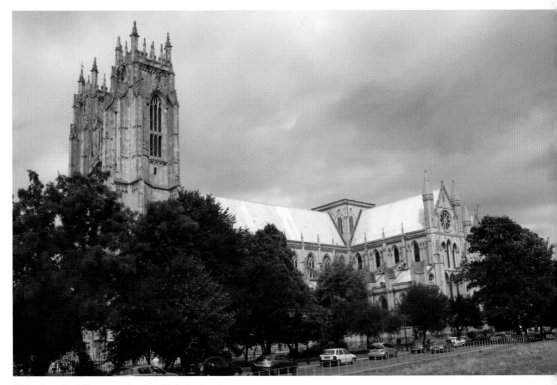

Above: Beverley Minster, on the site of John's church.

Left: Statue of John in Beverley Minster.

accounts of several such miracles, the beneficiaries of which included a sick, dumb peasant near Hexham, a critically ill nun at a monastery near Beverley, and a monk, Herebald (later to become Abbot of Tynemouth), following a fall from his horse in which he fractured his skull. Other miracles included the curing of a nobleman's servant who was so ill that a coffin had already been prepared for him, and a nobleman's wife who had been bedridden for three weeks. Although we have no evidence to support the suggestion, it may be that John understood a lot about medicine, and that his success in curing seriously ill people owed at least as much to his medical skill as it did to his prayers.

Archaeological excavations to the south of Beverley Minster in 1979-82 suggest that John's monastery was abandoned in the mid ninth century. This ties in with the traditional view that the monastery was sacked by Vikings in the ninth century, later to be refounded by King Athelstan of Wessex who in 927 became the first southern

The nave of Beverley Minster, with John's tomb in the foreground.

English king to assume control of the Yorkshire region. John was canonised in 1037 and his shrine at Beverley Minster (almost certainly on the same site as his original monastery) became a very popular pilgrimage site, and also an oft-used place of sanctuary for criminals and fugitives. Like Cuthbert, John was apparently very fond of animals, and it is said that in medieval times aggressive bulls and dogs became miraculously pacified when in the vicinity of his shrine. Today, John's unpretentious tomb can be visited in the magnificent setting of Beverley Minster, undeniably one of Britain's finest churches.

HERE LIES
THE BODY OF
SAINT JOHN OF BEVERLEY
FOUNDER OF THIS CHURCH
BISHOP OF HEXHAM A.D.687-705
BISHOP OF YORK A.D.705-718
HE WAS BORN AT HARPHAM
AND DIED AT BEVERLEY
A.D.721

John's tomb.

Anglo-Saxon frith stool (bishop's throne) in Beverley Minster.

9
St Benedict Biscop and St Ceolfrith

Born in 628 into a noble Northumbrian family, Benedict was a member of Oswiu's household until, aged 25, he joined the Church, accompanying Wilfrid to Rome in 653 and becoming a key player in the establishment of the Roman Church in Northumbria. He never became a bishop, but played an important educational role within the church, setting up the twin monasteries at Wearmouth (674) and Jarrow (682), both of which were endowed with extensive libraries and did much to stimulate the growth of Northumbria as a centre of learning. There were, of course, other monastic libraries in the kingdom, most notably at Whitby which was an acknowledged centre of learning under Hild, but the library at Wearmouth/Jarrow was apparently more extensive, containing volumes on a wide variety of subjects including Bible studies, history, medicine, astronomy, mathematics, literature and poetry.

Books at this time were very valuable, each one painstakingly hand-produced by monks in a scriptorium. Long before the introduction of paper, pages were of vellum (calf-skin) and the

Detail of original seventh-century doorway, St Peter's Church.

St Peter's Church, Monkwearmouth.

HE COLLECTS BOOKS IN ROME TO EQUIP A NEW MONASTERY

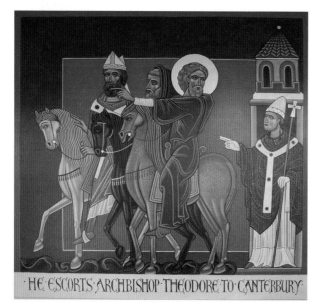

HE ESCORTS ARCHBISHOP THEODORE TO CANTERBURY

Two sections of a display at Bede's World, Jarrow, showing Benedict Biscop collecting books for his library and accompanying Archbishop Theodore on his journey from Rome to Canterbury.

production of a single decent bible could require in excess of 500 calf-skins. Although many books were bought in from elsewhere, or given as gifts (Benedict obtained many on his travels to Rome and Gaul), most were produced in-house; books would be borrowed from elsewhere and laboriously copied by monks. Many of these books were beautifully illuminated with colourful decoration, and were bound within intricately decorated leather covers, often embellished with inlaid jewels.

Benedict travelled to Rome six times; he was there in 668 when the much experienced and widely respected Greek monk, Theodore, was appointed Archbishop of Canterbury. Benedict accompanied Theodore on his journey to England, spending two years in Canterbury before returning back to Rome. Canterbury had a splendid library, which must have provided much of the inspiration behind Benedict's library at Wearmouth/Jarrow.

In 674, on returning from his

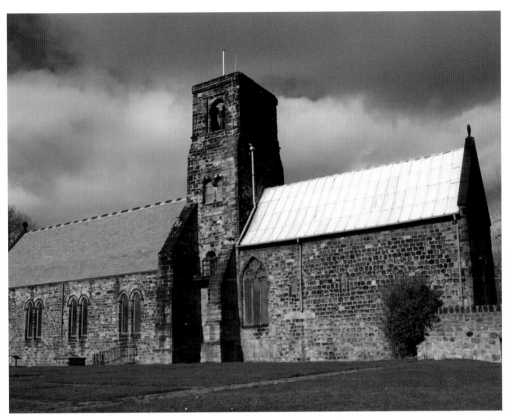
St Paul's Church: the section to the right was originally the smaller of Biscop's two monastic churches at Jarrow.

fourth trip to Rome, Benedict was offered land by King Ecgfrith to set up a new monastery at Wearmouth. Ceolfrith, a young monk with close links to Wilfrid, was appointed to help develop the new monastery. The monastery church, dedicated to St Peter, was built by craftsmen brought over from France. It was a fine structure, built of stone with glass windows. Benedict and Ceolfrith travelled to Rome and obtained a seal of approval for the new monastery from Pope Agatho, returning with many new books, paintings and relics. They also brought a Roman teacher to help instruct the monks in singing, chanting and reading. The new monastery continued to enjoy the direct support of Ecgfrith, and suffered none of the problems endured by Wilfrid and his monasteries at Hexham and Ripon.

In 682, Ecgrith gave Benedict a further grant of land for the establishment of a second monastery - St Paul's at nearby Jarrow. Ceolfrith led this project as Benedict was frequently away on his travels. Two churches (built using Roman

Cast of the original dedication stone in St Paul's Church. The inscription translates as: *The dedication of the Church of St Paul on 23rd April in the fifteenth year of King Ecgfrith and the fourth year of Ceolfrith Abbot and under God's guidance founder of this same church.* According to our modern calendar, the year in question is 685.

---

stone, perhaps pillaged from Hadrian's Wall or the fort at South Shields) stood end-to-end within the Jarrow monastery. The larger church, St Paul's, was dedicated in 685 and the original dedication stone still survives, built into the wall above the western tower arch of the present church. The smaller of the two seventh-century churches, possibly originally dedicated to St Mary, survives remarkably intact as the chancel of the present church (the rest of which was rebuilt in the eighteenth and nineteenth centuries). In 686, the Jarrow community was struck by plague and everyone except Ceolfrith and one young boy (possibly Bede) lost their lives. However, new monks were soon brought in and the community grew in strength, becoming one of the largest in England.

As we have already seen, Ecgfrith died fighting in Scotland in 685 and was succeeded by his half-brother Aldfrith, a keen scholar and lover of books. Although we have no direct evidence, we may reasonably assume that Aldfrith

Display of Anglo-Saxon stonework within St Paul's Church.

continued to support Wearmouth/Jarrow and the maintenance of the monastic library. Benedict died in January 690, having appointed Ceolfrith as Abbot of both Wearmouth and Jarrow, to be governed together as a joint institution with the maintenance of the library as a key priority. It is a great shame that nothing survives today of the Wearmouth/Jarrow library, one of the great libraries of the Anglo-Saxon world. However, it was much used by Bede, on whom so much of our understanding of the Golden Age depends, so we should not forget that we are indebted to Benedict and Ceolfrith, as well as to Bede himself, for this knowledge.

We know much about Ceolfrith thanks to the survival of an anonymous biography. In 716 he retired from his role as abbot and, aged about 75, set off for Rome, taking with him a beautiful, personally inscribed bible, produced at

Wearmouth/Jarrow, as a gift for the Pope. Sadly, he died before reaching Rome, but the bible (known today as the *Codex Amiatinus*) was delivered to the Pope and still survives today in a library in Florence.

The monasteries at Wearmouth/Jarrow were abandoned, like so many others, in the face of the Viking threat during the ninth century, but churches still survive at both, not only as fascinating archaeological sites but also as active places of worship. Both sites have seen extensive programmes of archaeological excavation which have uncovered many fascinating artefacts along with the foundations of the original monastic buildings. These excavations, alongside the historical accounts provided in Bede's *Lives of the Abbots of Wearmouth and Jarrow* and the anonymous *Life of Ceolfrith* provide us with a quite detailed overview of the Wearmouth/Jarrow community, which was certainly very wealthy. We know that in 716, when Ceolfrith set off for Rome, there were about 700 monks here, all living off the extensive estates originally provided by King Ecgfrith.

Intricately carved stone from St Paul's, Jarrow, showing two birds within a scroll, probably dating from about 700.

10
St Bede

Bede is one of the most important figures in the whole of British history. He was born in 672 or 673 on the estate of the Wearmouth monastery, entering the monastery at the age of seven. A couple of years later he transferred to Jarrow, where he lived for the rest of his life. Today, Bede's World, the Museum of Early Medieval Northumbria, stands adjacent to the site of the Jarrow monastery and demands a visit from anyone interested in the Golden Age.

In the monastic school Bede would have been taught reading, writing, Latin and Greek, as well as studying the Bible, all of which would prove essential to his later work. He became a deacon at the age of nineteen, and a priest at thirty. He was undoubtedly a devout Christian and rigidly observed the discipline of monastic life, but his greatest pleasure came not from preaching but from studying, writing and teaching.

Bede wrote more than sixty books, mostly in his own hand although he would have dictated to scribes on some occasions, especially as his health

Statue of Bede by Fenwick Lawson.

failed in later life. He wrote about many subjects, including Bible studies, history, chronology, natural science, poetry, grammar and language. Of particular relevance to Northumbria's Golden Age are his two Lives of Cuthbert, *A History of the Abbots of Wearmouth and Jarrow*, and his best-known work, the *Ecclesiastical History of the English People*, completed in 731 and dedicated to King Ceolwulf of Northumbria. Hundreds of copies of the Ecclesiastical History

Window in St Paul's, Jarrow, depicting St Paul, the Risen Christ, and Bede.

were laboriously hand-copied at scriptoria throughout Europe; the two most ancient surviving copies date from just a few years after Bede's death. The book presents the story of the development of the English Church and people from the Roman conquest through until the eighth century, with personalities and events discussed in chronological order. Of key significance is the use by Bede of the *anno domini* ('year of our Lord') dating system, whereby all dates are expressed as a number of years after the birth of Christ. This system had been developed in the sixth century but was not widely used prior to Bede, when dates were generally expressed according to a variety of cumbersome formulae relating to the reigns of emperors or kings. After Bede the new system was widely adopted, and is still in use today, despite the conveniently overlooked fact that no-one really knows for certain when Jesus was born!

The Ecclesiatical History is the key work for our understanding of the Northumbrian Golden Age. We must bear in mind, however, that Bede was not writing as an impartial historian, but as a committed Christian and an avid supporter of Anglian rule in Northumbria. His views of Northumbrian kings were clearly influenced by his Christian outlook. Oswald, for example, is presented as a kind and generous man and an ideal king, yet we know that kings at this time only maintained power through military strength,

Model of a monastic scribe and pupil: Lindisfarne Priory Museum.

Reconstruction of Jarrow monastery as Bede might have known it, by Peter Dunn.

frequently resorting to violence to expand their spheres of influence and reinforce their right to rule. We should also remember that a man is not necessarily a better man simply because he espouses Christianity; later history is littered with unsavoury characters who considered themselves to be Christians, while many undeniably good people followed alternative religious traditions. We may legitimately ask whether Bede would have thought so favourably of Edwin or Oswald had they not fought their battles in God's name, but should note that his Northumbrian bias enabled him to praise the pagan Aethelfrith ('a most mighty king') while demonising the Christian Cadwalla. He does so, however, by questioning Cadwalla's Christian credentials, stating that 'though a Christian by name and profession, Cadwalla had the temperament and character of a Barbarian.' The implication is that Cadwalla's actions were not those of a true Christian, but it is debatable whether his military tactics were in reality any less 'Christian' than those of Edwin or Oswald. In short, had Bede been born in North Wales rather than Northumberland then some of his opinions may have been rather different.

Another criticism often levelled at Bede is that he mixes accounts of historical 'facts' with miracles that most readers find implausible, leading some to question the historical reliability of his work. This is unfair. Bede was a product of his world, a pre-scientific world steeped in religious superstition within which the relics of saints really were associated with miracles. Just as miracles in the Bible

Bede by David Begbie: a thought-provoking exhibit at Bede's World.

were performed by Jesus and his disciples, Bede was concerned to present a number of 'local' miracles as performed by local saints but attributable ultimately to God.

Bede continued teaching and writing until his death, aged about 65, on 25th May 735. He was buried at Jarrow, but in about 1022 his relics were placed with those of Cuthbert in Durham Cathedral. Later, after the completion of the cathedral's Galilee Chapel in the late twelfth century, Bede was given his own tomb here, where he lies to this day. His work is extraordinary, both in its own right and because it laid the foundations for the development of the subject of history. Bede, for very good reason, will forever be known as the 'Father of English History'.

Bede's tomb in Durham Cathedral.

11
The Golden Age in the 21st century

Although it may have ended a dozen centuries ago, the Golden Age still exerts a powerful influence over the Northumbrian region today. People of a Christian persuasion will need no reminder of the importance to their lives of Cuthbert and the other saints featured in this book. For those who do not count themselves as Christians, the story of the Golden Age and the enduring influence of its art are nevertheless fascinating aspects of north-east history and culture. The emphasis placed by the ancient monasteries on knowledge and teaching is reflected in the

York Minster (left) probably occupies the site of Paulinus' original Northumbrian church, later completed by Wilfrid, while Durham Cathedral (above) was built to house the tomb of St Cuthbert. Now amongst the most famous churches in the world, neither would exist had it not been for the saints of the Golden Age.

Bamburgh Castle, the focus of the long-term Bamburgh Research Project which has uncovered much evidence dating from before, during and after Golden Age times. The excavation shown here is adjacent to Oswald's Gate, within the castle.

naming of Durham University colleges after Aidan, Cuthbert, Hild and Bede, while numerous other institutions, along with buildings, streets and other places throughout the north-east are named after the saints of the Golden Age. During the twentieth century, archaeological excavations at several sites have taught us much about everyday life during the Golden Age, and further research projects will no doubt have much more to tell us in future.

Many of the region's churches can trace their origins back to the Golden Age, and several of these feature decorated stonework of eighth or ninth century date.

Lindisfarne Priory, on the site of Aidan's monastery, is one of Northumberland's iconic tourist attractions and still a powerful pilgrimage destination for Christians.

Other churches incorporate more recent stonework displaying Golden Age influence, while many have stained glass windows depicting characters and scenes from the Golden Age. Many war memorials and funerary monuments are based on Golden Age crosses, and many modern artists and craftspeople produce works clearly influenced by the art of the Golden Age. At the time of writing, the Golden Age of Northumbria Project (in collaboration with which this book is published) is bringing together local community groups, archaeological projects, churches, schools, theatre groups and historical re-enactment societies to bring to life stories of the kings, saints and common people of early medieval

Above: The Lindisfarne Gospels Garden.

Below: Lindisfarne Heritage Centre.

Northumbria, while also encouraging people to explore the sublime landscapes and historic sites associated with the Golden Age.

Thousands of people each year enjoy St Cuthbert's Way, a long distance trail opened in 1996 running approximately 100km from Melrose, where the young Cuthbert began his religious career, to Lindisfarne, where he served as bishop and was originally buried. Also popular with walkers, St. Oswald's Trail runs some 150km from Lindisfarne along the stunning Northumbrian coast before heading inland through Coquetdale to Rothbury and on southwards to the site of the Battle of Heavenfield. Bede's Cycle Way runs for twenty kilometres between St Peter's at Wearmouth and St Paul's at Jarrow (linking the two sites which, despite the distance between them, were described by Bede as 'one monastery in two places'). These trails link Northumbria's magnificent landscapes and extraordinary history, and it is sobering to reflect that those using them are, at least in part, following the very routes taken by Cuthbert, Oswald, Bede and others featured in this book.

Some of the region's greatest tourist attractions owe their significance

Inspired by the stone crosses of the Golden Age, and standing in stark contrast to the surrounding industrial landscape of Tyneside, this fine Northumbrian Cross at Bede's World was designed and carved by Keith Ashford in 1997.

ultimately to the Golden Age. Chief amongst these are the magnificent cathedral at Durham (the best cathedral on planet Earth according to Bill Bryson) and the island of Lindisfarne, both of which have featured prominently in this book. Whether or not one considers oneself to be a Christian, it is a humbling experience to stand adjacent to Cuthbert's tomb, within the serenity of Durham Cathedral, while contemplating the story of the Northumbrian Golden Age. Other wonderful sites which demand a visit include York Minster, Beverley Minster, Ripon Cathedral, Hexham Abbey, Bamburgh Castle, Yeavering and the Farne Islands. In addition to these we must now add a more recent construction; Bede's World, the Museum of Early Medieval Northumbria at Jarrow. Here, adjacent to the site of Bede's monastery and the seventh-century Church of St Paul, visitors can enjoy a splendid exhibition about the Golden Age along with some full-size replicas of early medieval buildings and an Anglo-Saxon demonstration farm. Anyone wishing to find out more about Northumbria's Golden Age should begin by paying a visit to Bede's World, and follow this up with visits to many of the other sites featured in this book, perhaps even taking a few days out to walk all or part of St Cuthbert's Way or St Oswald's Trail.

The saints featured in this book lived in a world far removed from our own; a world in which superstition and religion accounted for much that we study today as 'science'. They aligned themselves firmly with Christ, and between them did much to ensure the subsequent dominance of Christianity over the lives of generations of Northumbrians. Today, science can indeed answer many questions, but there are many others that it cannot. Whether or not we choose to appeal to Christianity to help us answer these questions, we must surely regard the saints of the Golden Age with great respect. Regardless of our personal religious persuasions, these men and women have earned their place in our history. But the Golden Age is not just history; it has vast potential to enhance our economic, social and spiritual future. St Cuthbert may have been dead for thirteen centuries, but he still has a pivotal role to play in the future of Northumbria.

Images of Bede's World, the Museum of Early Medieval Northumbria.

Further reading

The following volumes should be of interest to readers wishing to learn more about St Cuthbert and the Northumbrian Golden Age.

Alcock, L. 2003. *Kings and Warriors, Craftsmen and Priests in Northern Britain AD 550-850*. Edinburgh: Society of Antiquaries of Scotland.

Backhouse, J. 1981. *The Lindisfarne Gospels*. Oxford: Phaidon.

Blair, P.H. 1976. *Northumbria in the days of Bede*. London: Victor Gollancz.

Brown, M.P. 2004. *Painted Labyrinth. The World of the Lindisfarne Gospels*. London: British Library.

Collingwood, W. G. 1927. *Northumbrian Crosses of the Pre-Norman Age*. London: Faber & Gwyer.

Cramp, R. 1984. *Corpus of Anglo-Saxon Stone Sculpture: County Durham and Northumberland* (2 vols). Oxford: Oxford University Press/British Academy.

Daniels, R. 2007. *Anglo-Saxon Hartlepool and the Foundations of English Christianity. An Archaeology of the Anglo-Saxon Monastery*. Hartlepool: Tees Archaeology.

Field, J. 2006. *Durham Cathedral. Light of the North*. London: Third Millennium.

Frodsham, P. & O'Brien, C. (eds) 2005. *Yeavering. People, Power & Place*. Stroud: Tempus.

Gallyon, M. 1977. *The Early Church in Northumbria*. Lavenham: Terence Dalton.

Hawkes, J. 1996. *The Golden Age of Northumbria*. Morpeth & Newcastle upon Tyne: Sandhill Press/Tyne & Wear Museums.

Hawkes, J. & Mills, S. (eds) 1999. *Northumbria's Golden Age*. Stroud: Sutton.

Higham, N.J. 1993. *The Kingdom of Northumbria AD 350-1100*. Stroud: Sutton.

Hope-Taylor, B. 1977. *Yeavering. An Anglo-British centre of early Northumbria*. London: HMSO.

Kirby, D.P. (ed) 1974. *Saint Wilfrid at Hexham*. Newcastle upon Tyne: Oriel

Marsden, J. 1989. *The Illustrated Bede*. London: Macmillan.

Marsden, J. 1992. *Northanhymbre Saga. The History of the Anglo-Saxon Kings of Northumbria*. London: Kyle Cathie.

O'Sullivan, D. & Young, R. 1995. *Lindisfarne*. London: Batsford/English Heritage.

Rollason, D. 2003. *Northumbria, 500-1100. Creation and Destruction of a Kingdom*. Cambridge: Cambridge University Press.

Sherley-Price, L. & Farmer, D.H. 1990. *Bede - Ecclesiastical History of the English People*. London: Penguin.

Stancliffe, C. & Cambridge, E. (eds) 1995. *Oswald: Northumbrian King to European Saint*. Stamford: Paul Watkins.

Webb, J. F. & Farmer, D.H. 1998. *The Age of Bede*. (Includes: Bede's Life of Cuthbert; Eddius Stephanus' Life of Wilfrid; Bede's Lives of the Abbots of Wearmouth and Jarrow; the Anonymous History of Abbot Ceolfrith). London: Penguin.

The Author

The author at Whitby Abbey
(Photo: Diane Anderson)

Paul Frodsham studied archaeology, anthropology and geography at the University of Durham, graduating in 1985. He worked as an archaeologist in Cumbria, London and Berkshire before being appointed as the Northumberland National Park Authority's first archaeologist in 1992. He was responsible for numerous important and popular projects during his time in the National Park, leaving in 2006. He currently lives in Weardale, County Durham, and is employed as the North Pennines Area of Outstanding Natural Beauty Partnership's Historic Environment Officer. He also runs his own consultancy, Oracle Heritage Services, dedicated to archaeological research, conservation and interpretation throughout northern England.

Paul has published numerous academic papers and popular articles and has written and edited several books including *Archaeology in Northumberland National Park, In the Valley of the Sacred Mountain – an Introduction to Prehistoric Upper Coquetdale, Yeavering – People Power and Place, and From Stonehenge to Santa Claus – the Evolution of Christmas*. In addition to archaeology, he lists his passions as his family, his library (which includes an ever-growing collection of antiquarian books about northern England), his garden (especially his collection of Japanese maples), and the study of philosophy.